Seeing Gray

Participant Study Guide

Seeing Gray
Where Faith&Politics Meet

Participant Study Guide

ABINGDON PRESS
NASHVILLE

Seeing Gray:
Where Faith & Politics Meet
Participant Study Guide

This book is printed on acid-free, elemental chlorine-free paper.

ISBN 978-1-426-70754-4

10 11 12 13 14 15 16 17 18—10 9 8 7 6 5 4 3 2
Manufactured in the United States of America.

Contents

Introduction

I came to faith in Christ as a teenager. I'd been away from church for years when someone invited me to a small Pentecostal church. A couple of years later, I felt God calling me to be a pastor. I entered a somewhat conservative college with very conservative and fundamentalist views. Although the school was no bastion of liberalism, it was there that I found myself stretched and many of my fundamentalist assumptions challenged.

I had lots of questions about faith, the Scriptures, and the "fundamental truths" I had been taught. I began reading the minor prophets and then the Gospels once again, and I began to see that God's call was not simply to tell others the good news, or even only that we have a "personal relationship" with him (as life-giving as this is). He also wanted us to do justice, to be concerned for the poor, and to provide help to those in need. I did not want to jettison what I felt was good in my Pentecostal experience—the personal relationship with Jesus Christ, a love of the Scriptures, and an emphasis on the work of the Holy Spirit. But I yearned for a church that would link these with a passion for justice, and where the intellect was valued as much as the heart.

My search led me to John Wesley, the eighteenth-century founder of the Methodist movement. His movement, Methodism, was born out of the theological conflicts that preceded him, and rather than finding himself drawn to the extremes, Wesley drew from them all as he articulated a gospel of the middle way. I joined The United Methodist Church when I was nineteen.

Joining The United Methodist Church meant that I would now need to attend graduate school in order to be ordained. I was

7

encouraged to attend a conservative seminary, but I felt that it was important to be exposed to the theological and biblical interpretations of a bit more liberal seminary. I opted for a school that was slightly left-of-center on the theological spectrum.

What I found by virtue of having attended a somewhat conservative college and a somewhat liberal seminary was an opportunity to listen to and explore the truth found on both sides of the theological divide. In the end I came to appreciate both theological liberals and conservatives. Both liberals and conservatives had important characteristics and theological positions that I found compelling. I began to wonder, "Are these my only choices? Am I either a liberal or a conservative? Or is there something in between?"

In the same way, an increasing number of Christians today are finding it difficult to identify with either side of this theological divide.

The results of a 2006 Pew Forum study of more than 2,000 Americans, entitled "Pragmatic Americans Liberal and Conservative on Social Issues," captures well the fact that a large number of Americans, regardless of the particular label they tend to claim for themselves, already see the world as a bit more gray than their labels would suppose. Researchers found that "Americans cannot be easily characterized as conservative or liberal."[1]

When people ask me, "Are you liberal or conservative?" my answer is usually, "Yes!" I see both liberal and conservative as two parts of a whole. When we say that someone is liberal with their giving, we mean that he or she is generous. I want to be liberal in that sense of the word! If *liberal* is defined as "favoring reform," that, too, captures my heart as a Protestant, because it recalls one of the important Reformation slogans, *ecclesia reformata, semper reformanda*: "the church reformed, always reforming." If *liberal* is a synonym for "broad-minded" or "open-minded" then yes, I wish to be a liberal!

Yet if *conservative* means holding on to what is good from the past, and being cautious in embracing change simply for the sake of change, then mark me conservative! If being conservative within the Christian community means retaining the historic doctrines of the Christian faith as articulated in the creeds, then I am conservative. If conservative means, as the Latin *conservare* does, guarding, keeping, or observing (presumably the treasures of the past), then, at least with regard to many things, I must be conservative.

On the other hand, if *liberal* means holding to the absolute right of individuals to do whatever they choose, or if *conservative* means simply seeking to maintain the status quo, I could not be defined as either liberal or conservative!

I might also respond to the person who asks me, "Are you liberal or conservative?" by noting, "It depends on who is asking." *Liberal* and *conservative* are relative terms and all but the most extreme among us are liberal relative to some people and conservative relative to others.

Even our most basic of ways of categorizing people in our society—left/right, liberal/conservative—point us to the truth that the world is not always black and white, and more often than not, we find ourselves somewhere in the gray between the two. It seems to me that increasingly there are large swaths of the Christian population who are yearning for a middle way.

As many Christians are drawn to a centered or balanced faith, there is an increasing frustration with the role that Christianity has played in the culture wars. Too often faith has been used by Christian leaders and politicians to further a particular political party or political agenda. And in the minds of many nonreligious people in America, Christianity is not associated with love or grace or justice, but with a particular view of homosexuality, or a particular stance on abortion, or a seemingly absurd and anti-intellectual view of human origins. Christianity has become a wedge that drives people from Christ, rather than drawing them to him. And Christians have, in their political involvement, acted to divide our nation rather than serve as the balm that can heal it.

There are a growing number of Christians who believe the gospel calls us to be healers and bridge builders, not dividers. There are new calls to civility in how Christians dialogue and debate ethical and political issues. And there are many Christians who are coming to see that even on the important ethical issues of our time there may be a need for a different approach than has been taken in the last thirty years.

In this book I attempt to lay out my view of a Christianity of the *via media* or middle way—a way that draws upon what is best in both conservative and liberal theology by holding together the evangelical and social gospels, by combining a love of Scripture with a willingness to see both its humanity as well as its divinity, and by coupling a passionate desire to follow Jesus Christ with a reclamation of his heart toward those whom religious people have often rejected. It is my intent to help us reflect together on how a "middle way" faith can and should influence and impact our culture, our country, and our world.

I believe our democracy rises or falls based upon the willingness of thoughtful people of conscience to get involved in the political process. Thus, the purpose of this book is to help us think about the important role of balanced faith in public life—about faith, morality, and politics and how we can see gray in these areas. Throughout the book we will be exploring three key questions:

- How can our faith lead us?
- How does our faith call us to be engaged in the public arena?
- And how do we do that in a way that's faithful to what Jesus taught?

I invite you to enter into the dialogue. You will agree with some points and disagree with others. I suspect that as time goes by, some of my own views will change. But as we seek to find a middle way together, recognizing that the world is not always black and white, we will come to appreciate its many shades of gray and to be the agents of love and grace God calls us to be.

Notes

1. See www.pewforum.org/docs/index.php?DocID=150.

The content of this *Seeing Gray Participant Study Guide* and the *Seeing Gray* DVD are drawn from a sermon series by Adam Hamilton. The series is based on his book, *Seeing Gray in a World of Black and White* (Abingdon Press, 2008). Five major themes from the book are covered here for use with small groups. For the full message and to continue your exploration of these issues, we invite you to read the complete book, *Seeing Gray in a World of Black and White: Thoughts on Religion, Morality, and Politics* (978-0-687-64969-3).

1. Where Faith and Politics Meet

1. Where Faith and Politics Meet

When he came to Nazareth, where he had been brought up, he went to the synagogue on the sabbath day, as was his custom. He stood up to read, and the scroll of the prophet Isaiah was given to him. He unrolled the scroll and found the place where it was written: "The Spirit of the Lord is upon me, / because he has anointed me to bring good news to the poor. / He has sent me to proclaim release to the captives / and recovery of sight to the blind, to let the oppressed go free, / to proclaim the year of the Lord's favor." And he rolled up the scroll, gave it back to the attendant, and sat down. The eyes of all in the synagogue were fixed on him. Then he began to say to them, "Today this scripture has been fulfilled in your hearing." —Luke 4:16-21

When we were children, most of us learned that there are two things one does not talk about among friends: religion and politics. This book discusses both. Both topics tend to generate strong views and passionate debates. Politics, in particular, can be a delicate subject. So, let me assure you that my goal is not to convince you to hold any particular religious or political views. Instead, it simply is to convince you that, as a person of faith, you should be involved in the political process. In fact, it is my belief that people of faith are essential to the political process.

Faith and Politics

Let us begin by considering the definitions of *faith* and *politics*. There are many different ways to define the word *faith*. For the purposes of our discussion, I am referring to our core values or beliefs—specifically, our beliefs about God, about what it means to be human, and about what is right and wrong. Even if you do not believe in God, you still have faith because you have core values and beliefs about whether or not there is a God, what it means to be human, and what is right and wrong. Once we understand that this is what faith is, we must ask ourselves this question: If I am not engaging these beliefs in the political process, what means and criteria am I using to make political decisions? You see, we simply cannot compartmentalize our faith, saying, "My faith belongs over here, and the life I live during the week belongs over there." Our faith is meant to influence every part of our lives—how we conduct business, how we treat our neighbors, how we interact with family and friends, and how we engage in politics.

Now consider the definition of *politics*. If you have taken any political-science classes in the last thirty years, you probably have encountered this definition of politics given by Harold Lasswell, a prominent political scientist and sociologist of the last century: Politics is the process for determining who gets what when and how. This definition of politics is about power, distribution, and control. If politics is indeed the process for determining these things, then it certainly requires some measure of morality—some sense of what is just and unjust. If you do not bring a sense of what is just and unjust—what is right and wrong—to the table when doing politics, then on what are you basing your politics? Are you taking a poll to see what the majority says before making any political decision? Of course, in a democracy the will of the majority is important, but it is not everything. There must be checks and balances because the majority might wish to do something that is unjust. This is why people of faith must be engaged in the political process—people who have a moral conscience, a sense of what is right and wrong, and who thoughtfully consider the issues.

In a speech delivered to the progressive evangelical organization Sojourners, Barack Obama said this:

> The problems of poverty and racism, the uninsured and the unemployed . . . are rooted in both societal indifference and individual callousness—in the imperfections of man. Solving these problems will require changes in government policy, but it will also require changes in hearts and a change in minds. . . . Secularists are wrong when they ask believers to leave their religion at the door before entering into the public square. Frederick Douglass, Abraham Lincoln, William Jennings Bryan, Dorothy Day, Martin Luther King—indeed, the majority of great reformers in American history—were not only motivated by faith, but repeatedly used religious language to argue for their cause. So to say that men and women should not inject their "personal morality" into public policy debates is a practical absurdity.[1]

Indeed, there is an undeniable connection between faith and politics.

Some Words of Caution

Having established the connection between faith and politics, it is important to offer some words of caution. When it comes to interjecting our faith into the political process, I would like to suggest three cautions—two on the side of involving our faith in politics, and one on the side of creating a clear separation of the two.

1. It is dangerous to use the language of faith as a cloak or means of excusing or justifying evil acts.

We've all seen or read examples of this. On September 11, 2001, the world watched as extremist Muslims flew airplanes into buildings, and the last thing they said as they did this was, "God is great." Likewise, Christians through the centuries have done many things in the name of Jesus that were evil and wrong.

The third commandment is the prohibition against misusing the name of God, and we tend to think this has to do with cussing. Certainly, that is an application of the commandment; but in the days when Moses gave the commandment, no one would have dared to say the name of God casually as we do today. Instead, the commandment had to do with speaking on behalf of God—claiming things that God never would have claimed. When we understand the commandment in this way, we see that there are two categories of people who most frequently violate the third commandment. The first is preachers, and the second is politicians. We must be wary when a politician begins to use religion as a way of rallying support for a particular position. The position may be consistent with the kingdom of God, or it may not. If we see that the position being advocated by using God's name actually hurts people, we should be greatly concerned.

A certain political figure once said, "My Christian feeling tells me that my Lord and Savior is a warrior. He calls my attention to the man who, lonely and surrounded by a few supporters, recognized what they, the Jews, really were, and called for a battle against them, and who by God was not the greatest sufferer, but was the greatest warrior." Do you know who said that? Adolf Hitler spoke these words in 1922 as he was advocating his Nazi party in the cities and villages of Germany.

To be sure, we must be discerning when people use religious language to advocate political positions. We must ask questions and critique their positions. They may be speaking the truth about what God would uphold, or they may not.

2. It is dangerous to oversimplify complex issues, being unwilling to question our own assumptions, biblical interpretations, and theology.

Often we want the world to be black and white. We want simple solutions to complex problems. We want a candidate to tell us in two minutes or less how he or she would solve the Social Security problem, deal with the environment, handle immigration reform, and ensure national security. Do you think you can solve these issues in two minutes? But that is what we want—two-minute answers. Actually, we want sixty-second sound bites that solve complex problems, and that is dangerous. There are people who are willing to give us sixty-second answers, and many of us gravitate toward those people—people who see the world in black and white. We must be willing to look for the answers on both "sides" and to realize that often the truth is somewhere in between. Unfortunately, we tend to want simple answers, and so we are prone to oversimplify. People of faith do this often. I encourage you to remember that your own views have changed over time. If you are growing in your faith and maturing as a human being, your views are going to change over time. Yet often we're looking for those simple views we had when we were teens or young adults.

In the last presidential election, the folks at CNN decided they would try to draw in younger viewers by allowing people to submit questions for the candidates via video on YouTube. There was a particular question related to religion that captures the essence of the oversimplification I am describing. It came from a man I will call Bob, and I will paraphrase his question to the candidates. He held up the Bible and said, "Your answer to this question will tell me all I need to know about you. Do you believe in this book?" The question I have is this: Is that really all we need to know in order to decide which candidate we will support for president of the United States? Besides, when it comes to biblical interpretation, there are a lot of places that are "gray"—places where we must use nuance and understand the complex ways people thought in the past and how we apply that in the present. We need to be people of faith who recognize complexity and think carefully about the issues rather than look for simple answers to complex problems.

Perhaps some visual examples can help to demonstrate the importance of recognizing complexity and seeing gray. For a very simple graph, a black line on a piece of white paper is sufficient. It is two-dimensional. It is what it is. Some issues are like that. There is a clear right and a clear wrong with no ambiguity or complexity at all. Most of life, however, is not like that. Consider a two-dimensional, black and white photograph of a field. Because there are no shades of gray, the photo simply does not capture the reality behind the picture. But if we begin to add a little gray to the photo, suddenly we can see the beauty and differentiate the sunflowers

from the field. We can see what a magnificent sight the photo represents because we are seeing shades of gray, not just black and white. Of course, the real world is much more than shades of gray. It is full of color, and that is where we find true beauty.

Some things *are* black and white, and so we see them in black and white. But so many things require us to recognize the complexity and the nuances in between. There must be people of faith who look at the questions and the complex issues from this perspective.

3. *It is dangerous to say there is no connection between faith and politics and thus divorce our faith from how we live our lives in the daily world.*

Some believe there is no connection between faith and politics. Their faith deals with spiritual things, politics with earthly things. The Bible is very clear that this view does not work in God's eyes. Throughout the minor and major prophets in the Old Testament, God repeatedly addressed this issue. The people thought they were doing God's will when they were keeping their religion private rather than living it out in the public arena, but God said that this was unacceptable. In Isaiah 58, the people were faithfully worshipping, praying, and fasting. Yet God had this to say:

> *Day after day they seek me*
> *   and delight to know my ways,*
> *as if they were a nation that practiced righteousness*
> *   and did not forsake the ordinance of their God;*
> *they ask of me righteous judgments,*
> *   they delight to draw near to God.*
> *"Why do we fast, but you do not see?*
> *   Why humble ourselves, but you do not notice?"*

Look, you serve your own interest on your fast day,
   and oppress all your workers. . . .
Will you call this a fast,
   a day acceptable to the LORD?
Is not this the fast that I choose:
   to loose the bonds of injustice,
   to undo the thongs of the yoke,
to let the oppressed go free,
   and to break every yoke?
Is it not to share your bread with the hungry,
   and bring the homeless poor into your house;
when you see the naked, to cover them,
   and not to hide yourself from your own kin?
Then your light shall break forth like the dawn
   and your healing shall spring up quickly;
your vindicator shall go before you,
   the glory of the LORD shall be your rear guard.
Then you shall call, and the LORD will answer;
   you shall cry for help, and he will say, Here I am. (58:2-3, 5b-9)

Politics is the process of determining who gets what when and how, and God has very strong feelings about these things. God says to us that we dare not divorce our faith from how we live out our lives in the daily world.

The Politics of Jesus

This leads us to consider the politics of Jesus. Many of us grew up thinking of Jesus as apolitical—that he was not involved in politics. Part of the reason we came to believe that is because we have not understood the political systems of Jesus' day. The political parties in Jesus' day were the Sadducees, Pharisees, Essenes, and Zealots. These were the groups that controlled the power when the Romans weren't controlling it. Jesus had a lot to say to these folks.

The overarching political power structure of Jesus' day was monarchy; that is, kings ruled over the land. The king of the area surrounding the Sea of Galilee was called Herod Antipas. Herod Antipas ruled at the will of God, as did all kings. He also ruled with the permission of the king of kings and the lord of lords, who in the first century was known to be Tiberius Caesar in Rome.

Jesus' Teaching and Healing Ministry

Understanding the political structure of Jesus' day helps us to see much of what Jesus said and did in a different light. For example, when Jesus taught his disciples to pray, he said, "When you pray, pray in this way. Thy kingdom come, thy will be done on earth as it is in heaven." That is a political prayer. Not only are we to pray that, we also are to do something about it—to work at it. Whenever we pray the Lord's Prayer, we are asking for God's will to be done on earth as it is in heaven. Then we are to work to fulfill that prayer.

Likewise, Jesus was making a political statement when he told the people to repent for the kingdom of God is at hand. He was not referring to the kingdom of Rome or the kingdom of Antipas. He told the people to repent and change their ways because *God's* kingdom was near. He not only said that the kingdom of God is upon or near you, he also said that the kingdom of God is within you. In other words, God is reigning and ruling as your king within you. He called people to become citizens of the kingdom of God first and foremost and then to live out their faith in God in all the other arenas of their lives.

Everything Jesus said and did unpacked this idea of the kingdom of God. As he went about ministering to people, he devoted most of his time to healing the sick. This was a political act. He was saying that in God's kingdom, God cares about the people who are sick. One time he stayed up all night long healing the sick. What does that tell us about God's concern for people who are sick? What might that tell us about the healthcare crisis in our world today?

Although Jesus' actions do not give us the answer to the healthcare crisis, it does tell us that God cares about the issue. God is concerned about the fact that there are children whose parents do not have insurance and are reluctant to take them to the doctor because they cannot afford it. God cares, and we should, too. What's more, our response must somehow be consistent with Jesus' response to sick people.

Jesus' Parables

Jesus also made political statements in many of his parables. He told one parable about a poor, destitute beggar named Lazarus who had sores all over his body. The dogs would come and lick his sores as he sat on the street outside the home of a wealthy man. Each day the wealthy man would walk past Lazarus and do nothing. Eventually, both of these men died. Lazarus went to the bosom of Abraham and received comfort for all the sorrows he had experienced in his life. The rich man ended up in hell. (See Luke 16:19-31.) This was a political parable about the kingdom of God. Jesus was demanding that people who are citizens of God's kingdom care about the poor.

In another parable, Jesus talked about sheep and goats. He said that on the last day those who will be consigned to hell will be those who saw the hungry and naked and thirsty and sick and imprisoned but did not do anything for them. (See Matthew 25:31-46.) Jesus was making a political point. We must look at the issue of welfare and recognize that although Jesus does not give us the answers in this parable, he does communicate that citizens of the Kingdom care about those who are in need.

In the parable of the talents, Jesus told the servants to be good stewards and take care of what the master entrusted to them while he was away for a time (Matthew 25:14-30). Perhaps this parable has something to say to us about how we take care of the earth God has entrusted to us. Likewise, in the parable of the good Samaritan, it is a foreigner—a Samaritan—who helps the injured Jewish man (Luke 10:30-37). Might this parable have anything to say to us about how we treat illegal immigrants? Or health care? Although Jesus' parables do not provide the solutions, they certainly tell us something about the kind of heart we should have.

Two Emphases: Salvation and Social Justice

There are two primary emphases in Jesus' ministry, and churches often divide along these lines. First, there is the emphasis on Jesus as personal savior. Some churches focus on salvation—the idea that we must be born again and have a personal relationship with Jesus Christ, that Jesus saves us from our sins and offers us everlasting life, and that Jesus walks with us and talks with us along life's narrow way. This is the foundational message of the Christian faith. It is the first part of the gospel message.

The second part of the gospel message is the call to holiness and action—the call to help the poor, to pursue justice and righteousness in the world, and to do God's will everywhere we go. Jesus said that we are to go into all the world and make disciples—to tell them to do the things Jesus commanded us to do. Some churches focus on this part of the gospel message. Mainline churches in the past century have emphasized the social gospel, concentrating on

25

social justice, Civil Rights, equal rights, the wrongful use of violence, and similar issues.

Both groups of churches have done great work, but sometimes they have forgotten the other part of the gospel message. Churches that focus on the salvation gospel have helped people to know Christ personally, but sometimes they have forgotten to tell them about the mission that Christ has saved them to carry out. Churches that focus on the social gospel have worked to bring justice and meet needs, but sometimes they have forgotten to tell people that they need a savior or to invite them to have a personal relationship with Christ.

We need to bring together both sides of the gospel; both are essential. We must love God with all our heart and we must love our neighbor as we love ourselves. This is the full gospel that Jesus preached: salvation and social action—personal holiness and social holiness.

A Challenge

In order for a democracy to work, thoughtful people of conscience must get involved. The ancients were not in favor of democracy. Both Aristotle and Plato said that a democracy would be a disaster because people could not be trusted to govern themselves. Even our founding fathers knew that a democracy was a risky experiment. They thought it would work, but they were not sure. So they built in some safeguards such as the Electoral College. Rather than the people directly electing the president of the United States, the Electoral College determines the outcome of a presidential election. The founding fathers were not sure that the people could be trusted to make right decisions every time.

If we are honest, we must admit that sometimes we are a bit silly in how we make our decisions. I have a friend who jokingly says that she voted for a particular presidential candidate because she thought he was handsome. I'm sure she had other reasons. The point I am making is that we must take seriously the issues facing our country and the qualities needed in our leaders. As people of faith, we must get involved. If we fail to do so, the consequences will be devastating.

So, I conclude this chapter with a three-part challenge.

First, get informed about the key issues facing our country. Determine what you consider to be the four most important issues facing our country today and explore possible solutions that are in keeping with the kingdom of God and the reign of Jesus Christ. Find out what political leaders on each side of the issue have to say, and come to a preliminary conclusion yourself.

Second, carefully examine every political candidate running for office. Examine their beliefs and their positions. Read articles, watch debates, and follow the news. Take the time to get to know who they truly are.

Third, if you have not already done so, register to vote and then exercise your right to vote. You have an opportunity and a responsibility to take seriously how you bring your faith to bear in the world as salt and light.

We need to be able to see the complexity and nuances in life and get involved as thoughtful Christian people. After all, our democracy rises or falls based upon the willingness of thoughtful people of moral conscience, conviction, and courage to participate in the political process. And that is the connection between faith and politics.

Notes
1. For full text of Obama's speech, visit: http://www.barackobama.com/2006/06/28/call_to_renewal_keynote_address.php.

For Reflection and Response

1. Why are faith and faithful people essential to the political process? How does our faith call us to be engaged in the public arena? How can we do this in a way that is faithful to what Jesus taught?

2. What does it mean to use religion as a cloak or a means of excusing evil acts? When have Christians done things that were evil or wrong in the name of Jesus?

3. Why is it dangerous for a politician to uses religion as a way of rallying support for a particular position? How can we know if a politician's position is consistent with the kingdom of God?

4. Why is it dangerous to oversimplify complex issues regarding faith and politics? Why is it important to be willing to question our own assumptions, biblical interpretations, and theology?

5. Do you agree that it is important to see the nuance between the black and white and realize that truth is not always on one side or the other but often somewhere in between? Why or why not?

6. Why is it dangerous to separate one's personal faith from one's public life? Read Isaiah 58:1-10. What can we learn from these verses regarding how God wants us to live out our faith in the public arena?

7. What can we determine about the politics of Jesus based on his words and actions? What did his ministry tell us about the kingdom of God, and how should this inform our involvement in the public/political arena today?

8. How can we bring together the two sides of the gospel—the salvation gospel and the social gospel—both as individuals and as a church body?

9. If a democracy is to succeed, why is it necessary for people of moral courage and conviction to participate in the political process?

2. Christ, Christians, and the Culture War

2. Christ, Christians, and the Culture War

Beloved, I urge you as aliens and exiles to abstain from the desires of the flesh that wage war against the soul. Conduct yourselves honorably among the Gentiles, so that, though they malign you as evildoers, they may see your honorable deeds and glorify God when he comes to judge. . . . As servants of God, live as free people, yet do not use your freedom as a pretext for evil. Honor everyone. Love the family of believers. Fear God. Honor the emperor. —1 Peter 2:11-12, 16-17

So often we view black and white as a metaphor for opposites that are in conflict with each other. The Chinese symbols yin and yang capture black and white as opposing forces that are at work against each other. They complement each other, but they are always opposites. This captures in some way what we find in the culture wars taking place in our world today. That is, there are forces in our society that are at odds with each other, and these opposing forces seem to feed each other. In the political realm we think of Republicans and Democrats, liberals and conservatives, right and left. The opposition between these forces or groups spreads out into the church and the world. The question we must consider is this: In light of this conflict, how should we, as Christians, engage our culture?

The Origins of the Culture War

The first person I know who used the term "culture war" to describe the conflict between the religious right, or moderate and conservative Christians who are identified with the religious right, and the left was Pat Buchanan. It was 1992, and he was hoping to seek the nomination for the Republican candidacy for president. Although he did not receive that nomination, he made a speech at the Republican Convention. In that speech he remarked, "There is a religious war going on in our country for the soul of America. It is a cultural war as critical to the kind of nation we will one day be as the Cold War itself." Buchanan spoke of a cultural war—of forces that were trying to push back opposing forces of darkness and restore some sort of "normalcy" or morality to our culture and country. Actually, this "war" had been going on formally for more than fourteen years by the time Buchanan offered these words.

To find the sources of the culture war, we need to go back to the 1960s, a time of great social, cultural, and political revolution in our nation. In a cover story appearing in *Newsweek* a couple of years ago, one writer commented, "The '60s are impossible to escape. They will define the 2008 presidential election, just as they have defined American politics, and American culture, for the last 40 years."[1] Perhaps a line from Charles Dicken's *Tale of Two Cities* describes it best: "It was the best of times, it was the worst of times."

There was great excitement and exhilaration across the nation in 1960 when President John F. Kennedy was inaugurated. The idealism of the young president was evident in his inaugural address when he declared, "Ask not what your country can do for you; ask what you can do for your country." Yet within a few short years, his life was snuffed out.

The Civil Rights Movement was an exhilarating and terrifying time. The Civil Rights Act of 1964 was a landmark piece of legislation outlawing racial segregation in schools, public places, and employment. Then, in 1965, the National Voting Rights Act outlawed discriminatory voting practices. The powerful speeches and sermons of Dr. Martin Luther King, Jr., were instrumental in helping to bring about these political victories. His famous "I Have a Dream" speech, delivered on the steps of the Lincoln Memorial during the March on Washington for Jobs and Freedom, clearly was a defining moment in the Civil Rights Movement. Tragically, just a few years later, his life, too, was snuffed out.

Only two months after the assassination of Martin Luther King, Jr., the nation was again jolted by another tragic assassination: Senator Robert (Bobby) Kennedy—the younger brother of John F. Kennedy.

During these tumultuous years, Lyndon Johnson initiated the Great Society, a set of domestic programs designed to eliminate poverty and racial injustice. The promise was a country that looked more like the kingdom of God than it ever had in the past. Yet, just as the legislation was being signed, so were the deployment orders for 550,000 young men and women who were going to fight and serve in Vietnam. Fifty-seven thousand of them never came back.

Nineteen sixty-one marked the advent of the birth control pill, and with it came a sweeping change in how people viewed human sexuality. There was a movement away from the view that sexuality is something precious that brings life and gives life to a man and a woman as they are joined together and made one flesh, to the view that sexuality is a casual, recreational activity. "Free love" was the new catch phrase.

Meanwhile, Timothy Leary was traveling across the United States advocating the legalization of LSD and marijuana and inviting people to "take a trip." This was touted as the new spirituality. *Newsweek* magazine announced what some theologians had already concluded: "God is dead." There were many who believed this idea.

As the decade progressed, there was a loss of credibility in government and an increase in popularity of the Women's Liberation Movement. This movement aimed at empowering women was exciting and exhilarating for some, bringing a new sense of freedom and opportunity for some and a sense of confusion for others.

By the end of the decade, divorce was on the rise. Between 1970 and 1975 the divorce rate in the United States rose 40 percent. My parents were divorced during that time period. Simultaneously, the marriage rate declined by 30 percent in that same five-year period, leaving people reeling and confused.

Perhaps the final straw leading to a backlash against all of this political, social, and cultural revolution was the court case Roe v. Wade. In this case, the Supreme Court determined that a woman had a constitutionally protected right to have an abortion for any or all reasons in the first two trimesters of a pregnancy. Because there is the chance that the unborn child could live outside the womb after the second trimester, states were allowed to restrict abortions during the third trimester, if they chose, except when the mother's life was in danger. In 1970, fifteen states had liberalized abortion laws and 200,000 legalized abortions took place. Nine years later, 1.5 million legal abortions took place in the United States.

The Reverse Pendulum Swing

Those who looked at Roe v. Wade as the final straw began to rise up, proclaiming that we had lost our way and something had to change. Groups began to form in the early 1970s, and in 1979 pastor Jerry Falwell formed an organization called the Moral Majority. The stated aim of the Moral Majority was to create a constitutional amendment, that would protect the unborn. If that couldn't happen, they wanted to see new judges appointed to the

Supreme Court who would be sympathetic to their cause and wish to overturn Roe v. Wade. Over time more elements were added to the platform. The Moral Majority quickly had millions of supporters, and they were very influential in the elections of 1980.

Soon other prominent individuals began to form new groups and add their voices to the cultural backlash, including Pat Robertson and the Christian Coalition and James Dobson and the Family Research Council. These political action groups lobbied and worked to mobilize voters to fight back the forces they had seen at work in the 1960s and early 1970s.

I have many friends in the religious right, but I do not subscribe to many of the positions they hold. In fact, I've distanced myself at a number of points. But I am grateful that they raised questions about the meaning of sexuality and have encouraged us to reclaim the idea that sexual intimacy is a sacred gift designed to bond people together so that the two might become one flesh. Likewise, I am grateful that they raised questions about pornography. I have seen too many men lose everything and end up in jail after becoming addicted to what they see on their computer screens, and I have seen too many children become addicted to pornography despite filtering software that their parents thought was working. So I'm glad that someone raised those and other important issues.

Even so, as they were raising these issues along the way, it seems that the pendulum swung farther and farther to the right, which is what tends to happen in societies. First, the pendulum swung far to the left in the 1960s, and then it swung far to the right in the 1970s and 1980s. Some people began to feel uncomfortable with this reverse pendulum swing. On some points the reaction seemed to be inconsistent with what Jesus himself stood for, bringing a whole new agenda with it.

When I think of the culture war, I think of Newton's Third Law of Motion which says that "for every action there is an equal and opposite reaction." If the 1960s went too far to the left, then the 1970s and 1980s seemed to go too far to the right. Many of us did not connect with the pendulum swing in the 1960s, but neither do we connect with reverse pendulum swing of the far right. Where do we fit?

Many of us find ourselves somewhere in the middle—with some of us leaning a little more to the right, some of us leaning a little more to the left, and some of us dead center. We see that there is good on the right and there is good on the left, and we find that often the truth falls somewhere in the middle—what Anglicans and Methodists called the *via media*, the middle way. So we are constantly looking at all sides of the truth in the light of the Scriptures—particularly in the light of Jesus' life, witness, and teachings.

Moving Beyond the Culture War

I believe it is time to move beyond the culture war. When I ask unchurched people to tell me why they do not go to church, they usually begin by saying, "You know, I like Jesus. It's Christians I don't like." When I ask why, they explain that Christians are hypocritical, judgmental, narrow-minded, and so forth. Where do they get that idea? Jesus wasn't that way, and most Christians I know are not that way. I believe they get this idea because some Christians who are very vocal *are* that way. These Christians see everything in black and white. They tend to be judgmental, harsh, and narrow, pointing out everyone else's sins. This causes people to turn away from Christ.

It is very important that we engage the culture as Christians, but it is equally important *how* we do it. Basically, we have four options when choosing how we will engage the culture. Let us consider each option and whether or not it is faithful to the example and teachings of Jesus.

Option 1: *Withdraw From the Culture*

Some Christians choose not to engage the culture, but instead to withdraw from it. The Amish are one example. By withdrawing from the culture, they are proclaiming that they do not fit in the culture. They are part of the kingdom of God, which is very different from the culture. They hold onto practices that go back hundreds of years, and in many ways life for them is very simple. It is a beautiful and admirable way of life. Yet this is not what Jesus did. Jesus participated in the world, associating with sinners. He did not withdraw but got involved.

Option 2: *Accommodate the Culture*

A second approach is to accommodate the culture, which means to adopt the practices of the culture. When we take this approach, we begin to look very much like the culture. Whatever the culture is doing, we do. The values of the culture become our values.

Perhaps with the exception of the Amish, every church or denomination or religious group I have seen has accommodated the culture in one way or another. Some of those accommodations are fine. Indoor plumbing, for example, is a good accommodation, as is air conditioning and a whole host of other things. But there are some things that are not good accommodations, particularly when it comes to our values. Often we adopt the world's values and then try to make Christianity fit into those values. All of us, myself included, have been guilty of accommodating the culture.

Option 3: Wage War on the World's Terms

Others take the approach of waging a militant war against the culture. This war is captured in the old gospel hymn "Onward, Christian Soldiers." The image of "marching out to war" is the sort of picture so prevalent in the culture war of recent years. The far right is depicted as fighting against the forces of evil in the world. This picture, however, does not look much like Jesus.

Certainly Jesus became angry at times, but he was never angry with the sinners in the world. Jesus did not go around blasting away at those who were known for sinful behavior. When Jesus blasted away, he was reprimanding religious people. *"Woe unto you, scribes and Pharisees, hypocrites,"* he said, because they were pushing away lost people rather than helping them become found (Matthew 23, KJV). This leads us to the fourth option for engaging the culture, which was modeled for us by Jesus.

Option 4: Provide a Courageous Witness Through Sacrificial Love

Jesus engaged his culture by providing a courageous witness through sacrificial love. As followers of Jesus, we should follow his example. This does not mean that we give up our values, saying there is no right or wrong. There is right and wrong. Rather, in the midst of understanding what is right and what is wrong, we must look carefully at how we live out and share that message.

I find the passage from 1 Peter, which appears at the opening of this chapter, to be instructive in this regard because it points to how early Christians were to live out their faith. Peter said to the Roman Christians, who were surrounded by pagans, *"Beloved, I urge you as aliens and exiles to abstain from the desires of the flesh that wage war against the soul"* (2:11). In other words, don't engage in the things all the people in the empire around you are engaging in, but conduct yourselves honorably among the Gentiles (non-believers). Why? *"So that, though they malign you as evildoers, they may see your honorable deeds and glorify God when he comes to judge"* (2:12). We are to live our lives in such a way that non-believers cannot say anything bad about us, even though they want to, because they see the good that we do.

Peter went on to say, *"As servants of God, live as free people, yet do not use your freedom as a pretext for evil. Honor everyone. Love the family of believers. Fear God. Honor the emperor"* (2:16-17). *Everyone* here refers to the pagans, because Peter later talks specifically about believers. In other words, we are to honor the people around us in the culture. We are to treat them with respect and care. Likewise, we are to honor and respect the leaders of our government. The emperor at the time Peter was writing was Nero, the most hedonistic emperor that Rome ever knew. Yet Peter instructed the Christians to show respect to the emperor. They did not practice a militant Christianity, waging war against the Romans. Rather, they understood themselves to be aliens and exiles from the kingdom of God living in a foreign land, and they desired to live such holy, honorable lives in that foreign land that people would be drawn to hear more about the gospel and to follow their way of life.

Changing the Dialogue

When it comes to the controversial issues involved in the culture war, I have found that there is truth on both sides. Think about it: There are huge numbers of people on both sides of most of these issues, and very seldom do you find huge numbers of people who are all idiots! Yet so often when we get into a discussion with those who believe differently than we do, we don't listen because we are convinced that we are 100 percent right and they are 100 percent wrong. Instead of listening, we think about what we will say next to beat them down with our position until they finally submit or give up. I've discovered that if I can sit with those who see the world differently than I do and simply listen—try to walk in their shoes and understand—I begin to see some of the truth in their perspective. When I listen with humility in this way, treating them with respect, they usually are open to actually hearing what I have to say. In the process, I find my own views are enriched and sometimes changed by virtue of having listened.

In the Book of James we read, *"Be quick to listen, slow to speak, slow to anger"* (1:19). Following this advice alone would help us to move beyond the culture war by changing the dialogue. We also would do well to listen to Jesus, who asked, *"Why do you see the speck in your neighbor's eye, but do not notice the log in your own eye?"* (Matthew 7:3; Luke 6:41), and to the apostle Paul, who said, *"In humility consider others better than yourselves"* (Philippians 2:3, NIV). Moving beyond the culture war involves walking with humility, practicing love, and listening with respect.

My hope is that we might become people who model a different approach to the Christian faith. When non-Christians look at us, I hope they will see our good deeds and say, "There's something authentic in these people." May we become salt and light in our society, always reflecting Christ's love.

Practicing Radical Love

I want to conclude this chapter with a story that illustrates how Jesus addressed sin in his culture. In the eighth chapter of the Book of John, we read that Jesus came down from the Mount of Olives and went to the temple courts. A crowd was listening to him teach when the Pharisees showed up. Remember that the Pharisees were pious religious leaders who focused on obeying the tenets of the Law and living the commands of God in righteousness. They came dragging a woman caught in the act of adultery, and they asked Jesus what they should do. They knew the law of the Old Testament said that anyone caught in the act of adultery was to be stoned to death. The stones were already in their hands. Jesus bent down before them and started to write with his finger in the dust on the floor of the temple courts. John doesn't tell us what he wrote, but the image of Jesus writing in the dust reminds us of God etching the Ten Commandments in stone. God was in the flesh among the people in the temple courts, writing with his finger. I like to think that either they saw what Jesus was writing or he told them what he was writing. Jesus stood up and looked at the Pharisees, who were so concerned with righteousness, and said, *"Let anyone among you who is without sin be the first to throw a stone at her"* (8:7). One by one, the stones dropped to the ground and they all walked away. All of the woman's accusers were gone, and there she sat with Jesus.

Bear in mind that Jesus had previously spoken about adultery. In the Sermon on the Mount, which occurred before this story took place, he had told the people that if they so much as looked at a woman with lust in their hearts, they would commit adultery against both her and God. Although this and other teachings of Jesus may seem rather harsh, we must interpret his teachings in light of how he lived them out. He made it clear that adultery is not God's will for our lives, but how did he interpret that for this woman?

Jesus lifted the woman up and said, *"Woman, where are [your accusers]? Has no one condemned you?"* She replied, *"No one, sir."* He said, *"Neither do I condemn you. Go your way, and from now on do not sin again"* (8:10-11). What I love about this is that Jesus was not contradicting his earlier teaching and saying that adultery is not a sin. Rather, he was telling her to live differently in response to his grace toward her.

Adultery is a sin, but that is not the dominant message of Jesus. The dominant message we hear from Jesus is grace. For me, this paints a picture of how we are meant to live our lives—how we are to engage the culture. We are to follow Jesus' example and live lives of grace, mercy, humility, and love.

What will we, as Christians, be known for today? My hope is that we will not be known as people who constantly blast everyone else for their sins, because we have our own sins. I hope that we will be known as people who practice acts of love and grace and service. I hope that we will be known as people who are humble, who listen, and who treat others with respect. I hope that we will be known as people who practice radical love. I believe that these are, in fact, the ways others will see us if we will strive to be people who see gray in a world of black and white.

Notes
1. See "1968: The Year That Changed Everything," Jonathan Darman, *Newsweek* (Nov. 19, 2007); www.newsweek.com/id/69637.

For Reflection and Response

1. How would you define or explain the idea of "culture war"?
2. How was the rise of the Religious Right a response to what happened in the 1960s and early 1970s? What questions did the

Religious Right raise, and what effects did this have in the culture?

3. What is the *via media*? Would you agree that the truth often is found somewhere in the middle—somewhere between the left and right? Why or why not?

4. Why is it important that we engage the culture? What are the four options we have for engaging the culture, and what do the teachings and example of Jesus say to us about each?

5. How does following Jesus' example draw others to the gospel?

6. Read 1 Peter 2:11-12, 16-17. According to these verses, how are we to live as Christians in the world?

7. What can help us to see the truth in the perspective of someone who sees things differently than we do? How can listening to others enrich and sometimes change us? How can our willingness to listen affect others?

8. Read John 8:2-11. What is the dominant message of Jesus in this story? What does Jesus' example teach about how we are to live our lives?

3. How Should We Live? The Ethics of Jesus

3. How Should We Live? The Ethics of Jesus

Just then a lawyer stood up to test Jesus. "Teacher," he said, "what must I do to inherit eternal life?" He said to him, "What is written in the law? What do you read there?" He answered, "You shall love the Lord your God with all your heart, and with all your soul, and with all your strength, and with all your mind; and your neighbor as yourself." And he said to him, "You have given the right answer; do this, and you will live." But wanting to justify himself, he asked Jesus, "And who is my neighbor?" Jesus replied, "A man was going down from Jerusalem to Jericho, and fell into the hands of robbers, who stripped him, beat him, and went away, leaving him half dead. Now by chance a priest was going down that road; and when he saw him, he passed by on the other side. So likewise a Levite, when he came to the place and saw him, passed by on the other side. But a Samaritan while traveling came near him; and when he saw him, he was moved with pity. He went to him and bandaged his wounds, having poured oil and wine on them. Then he put him on his own animal, brought him to an inn, and took care of him. The next day he took out two denarii, gave them to the innkeeper, and said, 'Take care of him; and when I come back, I will repay you whatever more you spend.' Which of these three, do you think, was a neighbor to the man who fell into the hands of the robbers?" He said, "The one who showed him mercy." Jesus said to him, "Go and do likewise." —Luke 10:25-37

In the previous two chapters, our discussion has focused on faith and politics. In this chapter, we turn our attention to ethics and morality. Ethics and morality go hand in hand. Morality is the accepted standard by which we determine what is right and what is wrong. Living morally is trying to live up to some standard that we consider to be right or normal. Failing to live up to this standard is what we call immoral living.

How do you determine what is right and wrong? What is the basis of the moral decisions you make in your personal life? Do the ethics of Jesus impact the way you live—the way you conduct your business, decisions, and daily activities? When it comes to the big issues facing our nation, how do you determine what is right and wrong?

For many of us, there seems to be little connection between the things that Jesus said and taught and how we decide these issues. We say that Jesus' ethics are the basis for the decisions we make, yet often we are unable to clearly articulate how the ethics of Jesus actually affect our decisions. The purpose of this chapter is to help us think carefully about how the ethics of Jesus impact our personal morals as well as our views on the big issues of our time.

Three Ways of Doing Ethics

Let us begin by recognizing that there are three primary ways of thinking about and doing ethics. The first two represent opposite ends along a spectrum, and the third represents a middle way.

1. Rules-based Ethics

On one end of the spectrum is rules-based ethics. This involves deciding what is right and wrong based upon a set of rules that some authority has given us. As people of faith, we say this authority figure is God. So, we determine what is right and wrong according to what God has told us is right and wrong. God has given us commandments or rules, and thus we are moral to the degree that we faithfully obey those commandments. Conversely, to the degree that we move away from those commandments, we are immoral. Of course, all of us fall short and have to call upon God's grace again and again. Nevertheless, a rules-based faith says that there are rules we must follow.

Although this makes some sense to us, we know that this form of ethics does not always work. For example, there are 613 commandments in the Old Testament, and another 800 commands in the New Testament. That gives us 1,413 rules. Even if it were possible to keep track of that many rules, we would run into some challenges if we were to take a close look at some of the rules. Consider the Old Testament commandment that says if your children are disobedient, you should stone them to death. As a parent of teenagers, there have been times when I momentarily thought that might be a good idea! But seriously, if we tried to live out that commandment today, we would be considered immoral and would be arrested. Clearly, as we look at some of the commandments, we realize that a little interpretation and understanding are necessary before blind obedience.

Another problem that arises with rules-based ethics is that there are never quite enough rules for every life situation. When you are choosing what is right or wrong based upon pre-determined rules, what happens when there isn't a rule for your particular life situation? You come up with another rule! That is how the Jews of the Old Testament wound up with 613 rules, and those rules still were not enough. So they came up with additional rules, and these rules became part of the oral law that eventually was written down in the Talmud.

Consider the fourth commandment, for example: *"Remember the sabbath day, and keep it holy. . . . you shall not do any work—you, your son or your daughter, your male or female slave, your livestock, or the alien resident in your towns"* (Exodus 20:8, 10). That seems straightforward, but is it? What, specifically, am I supposed to do to keep the sabbath holy? The commandment doesn't say. You might say that I am not supposed to work on the sabbath, but what constitutes work? In light of questions such as these, the Jews came up with all kinds of additional regulations for the sabbath, such as no cooking, no walking more than so many yards, no carrying a needle, and so forth. If you go to the Holy Land today, you will find that the hotel elevators are programmed to stop on every floor on the sabbath day because pushing a button is considered work.

One rule leads to more rules, and pretty soon you get stuck on all the rules. Anyone who has children or works with children knows that you simply cannot come up with enough rules to cover every situation. Just when you think you've done your best to cover all the bases, they find some way to slide right by the rules, saying, "You never told me not to do that." We respond, "Well, do I have to tell you everything?" With a rules-based ethic, the answer is yes.

In the Gospels we see that Jesus was regularly confronted by the rules-based folks of his day. Although he did not dismiss the idea of rules, he clearly did not follow the letter of the law in every situation. As we saw in the previous chapter, the law said that anyone caught in the act of adultery was to be stoned to death, yet Jesus showed an adulterous woman grace. He continually got into trouble with the Pharisees because he often broke their rules. He didn't wash ceremonially before he ate his meals. He violated sabbath rules. He ate plucked grain on the sabbath. He healed on the sabbath. When the Pharisees confronted Jesus about these infractions, he made it clear that the sabbath was made for people, not vice versa. Therefore, if someone was sick and hurting on the sabbath, he healed them because the important thing was helping others, not following the rules. Jesus did not throw out the rules, but he chose to be reasonable about them.

2. Outcomes-based Ethics

On the other end of the spectrum is outcomes-based ethics. We also might call this consequence-based ethics. According to this way of doing ethics, no activity is moral or immoral in and of itself. It is the outcome that determines whether something is moral or immoral. If I do something that hurts someone else, the act is immoral in that given situation because it hurts someone. But if I do the same thing in another situation and it helps someone, then the act is moral in that situation.

Outcomes-based ethics is a very popular way of doing ethics, but it has its problems, too. In the 1960s, the outcomes-based ethic mantra was "If it feels good, do it." Just because something feels good, however, does not mean that we should do it. We know there are many things we shouldn't do even though they feel good.

There is a utilitarian concept in outcomes-based ethics that is very pragmatic. When taken to the extreme, this view says that the end justifies the means. Most of us would say that idea is not right, acknowledging that some means are so evil that it doesn't matter how good the ends are; some things are just wrong. For example, what if I were to say that a thousand people could be saved from death if we were to take the blood and organs from just one healthy person? Most of us, I hope, would say that it is wrong to force someone to give up his or her life, even though good would result. Why? The ends do not justify the means.

At first glance it may seem that Jesus sometimes practiced outcomes-based ethics, such as when he healed on the sabbath. The end seemed to justify the means. But when we look closer, we see that Jesus actually took a stand somewhere between the two extremes—between rules-based ethics and outcomes-based ethics. He did not give up the rules, but he also intentionally considered the outcome. By his example, he showed us that there is a balance between the two—a gray area or middle ground. We will call this middle ground virtues-based ethics.

3. Virtues-based Ethics

Virtues-based ethics involves making decisions based on a set of virtues or values. In every situation, you try to do what those virtues call you to do. As followers of Jesus Christ, we look to the virtues of Jesus when making decisions. Jesus was compassionate and taught us to be compassionate. So, whenever we see someone who is hungry or thirsty or in need, we do something about it. That's a virtues-based ethic.

Jesus also told us to serve one another and love one another and forgive one another. Serving and loving and forgiving or showing mercy are all virtues. As followers of Jesus, we choose to do the things that allow us to live into these virtues. That's a virtues-based way of doing ethics.

Virtues-based ethics is tied to a set of virtues, which is well and good if the virtues are sound. However, this method of doing ethics can be problematic if the source and selection of the virtues are not trustworthy and true. Like the other two ways of doing ethics, this one falls short of possessing all truth in and of itself. It is only when this method of doing ethics is tied to the person and life of Jesus Christ, who is Truth, that it becomes fully trustworthy and true.

Our Central Ethical Principle: Jesus Christ

As Christians, we are called to follow Jesus Christ as our Lord. In other words, we are to do those things that Jesus wants us to do. This means that we must look to his example and his teachings, trying to live according to the precepts that he taught and lived. So, when it comes to deciding what is right and wrong, our central ethical principle is Jesus Christ. Our goal is to live the way that Jesus lived.

As followers of Jesus Christ, we are to give our lives to him each day. Every morning when I wake up, I get on my knees next to my bed, lift my hands up to the Lord, and say, "Jesus, help me to follow you today. Help me to honor you and live for you and please you. Help me to live the way you want me to live. I offer my life to you once more today." Many of us say that we surrender our lives daily, yet the choices we make and the way we live do not reflect the values that Jesus taught and lived. Gandhi commented on this once. He was intrigued by Jesus and liked the things that Jesus said, but when he looked at Christians, he did not see much evidence that they lived out their faith. He said that everyone seemed to know what Jesus said except Christians.

Sometimes it does seem that Gandhi's observation is accurate. Though we are Christians, our views are often shaped by a variety of things other than Jesus Christ. Our views on the big issues of our day, for example, might be shaped by our favorite talk show host or newspaper columnist, by some movie we saw, or by what our parents said. As Christians, however, our views should be shaped first and foremost by Jesus Christ.

In his book *The Red Letter Christians: A Citizen's Guide to Faith and Politics*, Tony Campolo looks at twenty key issues facing our nation today through the lens of the things that Jesus said. The title plays upon those versions of the Bible in which the words of Jesus appear in red. Campolo says that as Christians, we should look at those red letters and give them supreme authority in our lives. The Word of God became flesh in Jesus Christ. Thus, the words of Jesus were the very words of God—the only time when God's words were not mediated through prophets or lawgivers or apostles. What Jesus said and did is the lens through which we are to understand every other part of the Bible, as well as the issues confronting us today. Although Jesus did not talk directly about any of the twenty issues highlighted in the book, Campolo considers how the things that Jesus did say can shape our views today. We may disagree with some of what Campolo says, but the important thing is that he shows how we can relate Jesus' words to what is happening in our world. We are to be red-letter Christians—people who try to actually live out the things that Jesus said.

Three Simple Rules

So, what *did* Jesus say? When Jesus gave the Sermon on the Mount, he was speaking to common folk. They did not have degrees in ethics or philosophy. They did not understand deontological ethics or teleological ethics. They just wanted to hear how they were supposed to live. So Jesus gave them three simple rules to live by—three basic precepts. He did not expect the people to memorize 1,413 laws. Instead, he said that the law and the prophets could be summarized in these three simple rules. With each rule, I would like to suggest one or two corresponding questions that we can ask ourselves when making moral decisions.

Rule 1: *Love the Lord your God with all your heart, and with all your soul, and with all your mind. (Matthew 22:37)*
Question: *Will this honor God?*

Jesus said that this is the greatest and first commandment. When it comes to morality and ethics, what does it mean to love God with all our heart, soul, and mind? It means that we are to honor God in everything we do. Our lives—all that we say and all that we do—are to express the love of God and our love for God. It means that before every decision we make and every action we take, we must ask ourselves this question: "Will this honor God?" In other words, will the political position we adopt or the moral decision we make or the specific course of action we choose be a reflection of God's love and our love for God?

Rule 2: *Love your neighbor as yourself. (Matthew 22:39)*
Question: *What is the loving thing to do?*

The second great commandment that Jesus gave us is to love our neighbor as we love ourselves. This was the central ethical principle of Jesus' teachings. He said that not only are we to love our neighbor; we also are to love our enemy and pray for those who hate us or wrongfully abuse us (Luke 6:27-28). We are to let the world know that we are his disciples by the love that we have for one another (John 13:35). Jesus said, *"No one has greater love than this, to lay down one's life for one's friends"* (John 15:13). Similarly, at the end of the Gospel of John, Jesus showed his disciples the full extent of his love by getting on his knees and washing their feet—and later being crucified for them. Indeed, love was the organizing principle of Jesus' ethics.

In the 1960s, an Episcopalian priest and ethicist named Joseph Fletcher devised a whole system of ethics around this idea of love, and it is called situation ethics. It has some major shortcomings, but I like the question that Fletcher suggested we ask ourselves in every situation: "What is the loving thing to do?" In every conversation, what is the loving thing to do? In every business transaction, what is the loving thing to do? In every situation involving coworkers or employees or family members, what is the loving thing to do? In every national issue or concern, what is the loving policy that we might pursue?

Rule 3: Do to others as you would have them do to you.
Questions: How would I feel if I were in the other person's shoes? What would Jesus have me to do in this situation?

Jesus gave us a third principle that he said summarized the law and the prophets. We find it in the Sermon on the Mount: *"In everything do to others as you would have them do to you; for this is the law and the prophets"* (Matthew 7:12). We call this the Golden Rule, and many of us learned this rule when we were children. Basically, it means that we need to walk in the other person's shoes if we want to determine what is right or wrong in a particular situation. This principle applies across the board, from personal situations to political situations. If we are selling a used car, for example, we need to ask ourselves what it would feel like to be on the other side of the transaction. Would we feel good about the car after driving it for a month or two? Likewise, in a relationship with a boss or a spouse, we should ask ourselves how we would feel if the other person were treating us the way we are treating him or her. Would we feel good about being treated that way? Or in matters of foreign policy, we need to ask ourselves if we would want this particular nation to treat us the way we are treating them. Whatever the situation might be, we need to walk in the other person's shoes for a little while.

My wife, LaVon, has taught me how important it is to walk in the other person's shoes. Some years ago we were in the midst of a really busy time at the church. I had meetings every night for two weeks. At the end of those two weeks, LaVon pointed out that I was never home anymore. So I promised I would leave my meeting early that evening and come home. She said, "Great. I'll make dinner and we'll have a nice evening together."

That night during the meeting, things began to heat up, and we got into a really involved discussion. I couldn't walk out—not even to make a phone call. As the senior pastor, I simply had to be there. An hour later, I finally walked out of the meeting, arriving home an hour late. LaVon looked at me and said, "I just want to ask you one question. If I had been at work every night for two weeks and then I promised you that I would be home at a certain time, and if you had made a nice meal for us and then I showed up an hour late and didn't even call, how would you feel?" I realized then that I needed to walk in her shoes.

Walking in another person's shoes was an important organizing principle of ethics for Jesus. The question that relates to this organizing principle of ethics is this: "How would I feel if I were in the other person's shoes?" Another way of coming at this question might be to ask ourselves, "What would Jesus do if he were walking in my shoes?"

In 1896, a pastor by the name of Charles Monroe Sheldon wrote a fictional book called *In His Steps*. In this book he tells the story of a homeless man who walked into a Midwestern church and was ignored by the congregation. No one showed him any compassion. In the middle of the service, he stood up and began to preach to the people. He told them that although they talked about how much they loved Jesus, it was hard to see it. They didn't do the things that Jesus said we are to do. After he chastised them, he sat down; and before the service was over, he died right there in their midst. It was most unnerving for the people. The next week the pastor told the congregation that something had to change. He challenged them to ask themselves this question in every situation for one year: "What would Jesus do?" So, for one year the people of that congregation did just that. Although the townspeople ridiculed them, they would not stop asking the question; and the lives of everyone in the town were dramatically changed as a result.

What would Jesus do? is still a great question to ask when we're walking through life. A number of years ago the abbreviation for this question, WWJD, appeared everywhere on wristbands and T-shirts and other personal items. Perhaps an even better question to ask ourselves—because we are not Jesus but are his followers—is this: "What would Jesus have me to do in this situation?"

This question—along with the other questions I have suggested—is helpful in terms of forming our own sense of what is right and wrong—what is moral and immoral. But the problem is that we are the ones who are coming up with the answers. After all, we are the ones thinking about what we think Jesus would have us do! So, the question becomes: "Is there a good way to determine the answers?"

John Wesley's Quadrilateral

The answer is yes. John Wesley, the founder of Methodism, developed what is known now as the Wesleyan Quadrilateral—four bases of authority by which we can answer important questions such as the ones we have been considering. Let us consider each leg of the quadrilateral separately.

1. Scripture

Wesley said that we are not to come up with answers on our own. Rather, we are to study the Bible and learn the principles that are found in the stories of Scripture. This helps us to determine and understand the answers to important questions regarding faith and life. Wesley recognized, however, that Scripture must be interpreted, which is why he looked to the church—to tradition—to help in this regard.

2. Tradition

For Wesley, tradition referred to what Christians through the ages have believed about the Scriptures. When applying this leg of the quadrilateral, we are to ask ourselves what theologians, ethicists, and pastors say about the Scriptures—how they interpret them. We also should ask ourselves, "What do the people in my church and study group say about the Scriptures? How can they help me understand the Scriptures and apply them when answering important questions?"

3. Experience

When Wesley talked about experience, he was referring specifically to the experience of the Holy Spirit. Jesus said, *"When the Spirit of truth comes, he will guide you into all the truth"* (John 16:13). Wesley believed that if we learn to listen to the voice of the Holy Spirit, the Holy Spirit—along with the church and the Scriptures—will guide and help us to understand the answers to the questions we are asking.

4. Reason

The last leg of the quadrilateral is reason. Although Wesley counted this as the least reliable of the four sources of authority, he said that God gave each of us a mind for a reason. We are to use our ability to think and reason as we listen to the voice of the Holy Spirit, to the church, and to the Scriptures. Together these things can help us to answer the important questions *Will this honor God? What is the loving thing to do?* and *What would Jesus have me to do?*

A Picture of the Ethic of Love

As we look to the Scriptures, tradition, experience, and reason to answer questions and make moral decisions, we do well to remember that the central ethic of Jesus is love. We can be certain that the right, moral choice will never contradict this central ethic of love.

No story captures the ethic of love more beautifully than the parable of the good Samaritan. No doubt you are familiar with the story. Even if you did not attend church when you were growing up, you probably have heard the term "good Samaritan." The origin of this term is found in this story.

Jesus told the story in response to a lawyer who came to him one day and said, *"Teacher . . . what must I do to inherit eternal life?"* (Luke 10:25). Essentially the lawyer was asking, "What does the moral life look like? What do I need to do to be good?" Jesus asked the man what he thought was the answer, and the man said, *"You shall love the Lord your God with all your heart, and with all your soul, and with all your strength, and with all your mind; and your neighbor as yourself"* (v. 27). Jesus replied, *"You have given the right answer; do this, and you will live"* (v. 28). Lawyers tend to want to nail things down, so the man came back with this question: *"Who is my neighbor?"* (v. 29).

Basically, the lawyer was asking, "Whom do I *not* have to love? To whom does this rule *not* apply?" Jesus answered by telling a story.

A man—a Jew—was going down from Jerusalem to Jericho. This was a very dangerous road at that time. There were thieves all along the road, and there was a pass called "the bloody pass" where people often were accosted. People did not want to travel this road alone—and certainly not at night. As the man was traveling alone along this road, he was robbed, stripped naked, beaten, and left for dead.

A priest came along and saw the man on the side of the road. Assuming that he was dead, the priest walked around to the other side and continued his journey down to Jericho. Next, a Levite, a religious professional, came along. He saw the man and assumed he was dead. Or perhaps he thought that it was a trap and that thieves would accost him if he stopped. So he crossed to the other side of the road and made his way down to Jericho. Finally, a most unlikely hero came along: a Samaritan. The Jews considered the Samaritans to be a different race, second-class citizens, and heretics. Good Jews wouldn't even walk through Samaritan territory. Yet this Samaritan got off his donkey, bound up the wounds of the injured man, and placed him on the donkey. Then the Samaritan took the man to Jericho and provided for his shelter, food, clothing, and care.

Jesus asked, *"Which of these three, do you think, was a neighbor to the man?"* (v. 36). The lawyer answered correctly, saying that it was the one who helped the man. Jesus said simply, *"Go and do likewise"* (v. 37).

It is easy to condemn the priest and Levite for what they did and did not do in the story. However, according to Leviticus 21:11, if you even were to touch a corpse, you would be unclean for seven days. The priest knew that he would need to cancel all his appointments for the next seven days if he touched the man. Let me ask you a question. If you saw someone lying on the side of the road, would you stop and help the person if it meant canceling all of your appointments for the next seven days? Or would you think that maybe someone else would come along and help that person?

Let's say that you are willing to make that sacrifice. Then you realize that the man will have to ride on your donkey and you will have to walk the twenty-three miles to Jericho. So, how are your walking shoes today? How are your knees or your hips? Remember, this is a man you have never met before and know nothing about. Are you going to give up your appointments for the next seven days and walk twenty-three miles for someone you've never met before, or are you going to count on the fact that someone else will come by after you and take care of the problem?

Let's say that you are willing to cancel your appointments for seven days and walk twenty-three miles. Then you remember that there are no free inns in Jericho. The man has no money. Everything has been taken from him. He is naked and in need of clothing. He will need food and health care as well. You begin to wonder what it will cost to take care of his needs, and you determine that it will cost two denarii, which is two days' worth of wages. What do you make in a day? The average daily wage in my city is about $200. In other cities it is as much as $500. Are you going to cancel your appointments for seven days, walk twenty-three miles, and spend up to one thousand dollars of your own money? Will you stop to help, or will you count on the fact that someone else will come along and take care of the problem? Be honest. Actually, I do not think that the priest and the Levite were that much different than you and me.

Ironically, the one who stopped to help was the one with whom there was racial tension; the one whose theology was considered bad; the one who had been pushed down by the Jews. Jesus was saying that the condition of your heart is more important than your theology or social standing. He was saying that love is found in what you do for people who are hurting. Love is found in sacrifice. The good Samaritan is a beautiful picture of what the ethic of love looks like.

Martin Luther King, Jr., no doubt preached on this parable more than once, but the last sermon he ever preached happened to be on this passage of Scripture. King had gone to Memphis, Tennessee, to stand with the sanitation workers, both black and white, who were the working poor. No matter how hard they worked, they couldn't make a living to support themselves. So they had gone on strike, and nobody seemed to care. King wanted to add his voice to their cry for help and relief. He was not feeling very well that night. He was worn out, and he almost did not go to speak. But he wanted to be there for these people, so he went. He knew there had been death threats against him, but he went anyway.

The conclusion of the sermon King preached that night is often quoted. King said that it wouldn't matter if he died, because he had been to the mountaintop and had seen the other side. He said that his eyes had seen the glory of the coming of the Lord. But before this famous part of the sermon, he preached on the parable of the good Samaritan. He said that the first question the Levite and the priest asked was this: "If I stop to help this man, what's going to happen to me?" Then the good Samaritan came by and reversed the question. He asked, "If I don't stop to help this man, what's going to happen to him?" King told his listeners that this was the question before them that night—not, "If I stop to help, what will happen to me?" but "If I do not stop to help, what will happen to them?"

As followers of Jesus Christ, this is the question we must ask ourselves on a daily basis: "If I don't do anything, what's going to happen to them?"

A Challenge

Once again I close the chapter with a challenge. Be a red-letter Christian. Get serious about living out your faith, taking it to the streets. Every day ask yourself, "Will this honor God? What is the loving thing to do? What would Jesus have me to do in this situation?" Live your life so that others look at you and say, "That person is trying to change the world! He/she looks like Jesus." That is my hope and prayer for you and for me.

For Reflection and Response

1. What are three ways of doing ethics? How would you describe each method? Think of an example of each.
2. Why is each of these approaches to morality inadequate in and of itself? What are some of the problems with these approaches?
3. What does it mean to be a "red-letter Christian"? Why are we to attach supreme value to the teachings of Jesus—even above other parts of the Bible?
4. What three basic precepts or rules did Jesus give us to live by?
5. Based on these three rules, what are the questions we should ask ourselves when making moral decisions and choices?

6. What is the Wesleyan Quadrilateral, and how can it help us to answer questions when making moral decisions and choices? Why are all four legs of the quadrilateral important? What happens when we exclude any of them?

7. Read Luke 10:25-37. Why do you think the priest and Levite chose not to stop and help the injured man? Which of the three approaches to morality do you think they used to reach this decision? Why is the Samaritan an unlikely hero? How did his actions demonstrate sacrificial love?

8. What question did Martin Luther King, Jr., say we should ask ourselves when determining whether or not to get involved and help others in need? How did his own choices in his last days reflect the fact that he practiced what he preached?

4. Spiritual Maturity and Seeing Gray

4. Spiritual Maturity and Seeing Gray

At that time the disciples came to Jesus and asked, "Who is the greatest in the kingdom of heaven?" He called a child, whom he put among them, and said, "Truly I tell you, unless you change and become like children, you will never enter the kingdom of heaven. Whoever becomes humble like this child is the greatest in the kingdom of heaven. Whoever welcomes one such child in my name welcomes me." —Matthew 18:1-5

If I speak in the tongues of mortals and of angels, but do not have love, I am a noisy gong or a clanging cymbal. —1 Corinthians 13:1

Throughout this book we have been considering what it means to see gray in a world of black and white—and how this affects the way we live out our faith in the world. Seeing gray involves finding common ground with those who disagree with us and embracing them with the love and grace of Jesus Christ. This requires spiritual maturity.

What Is Spiritual Maturity?

Spiritual maturity is a term that is tossed around loosely in Christian circles, but what is it? Simply put, spiritual maturity is characterized by trust and love. The lives of those who are spiritually mature are defined by these two characteristics. In this chapter we will look at these characteristics of spiritual maturity and how they contribute to a balanced faith. We also will explore the divisions and complications that result when we lack spiritual maturity and insist on rigidity and certainty.

Let us begin with trust. Individuals who are spiritually mature trust with childlike faith. This kind of trust does not come naturally. Our human bent is to want certainty. We may think that we like to live in the gray areas, but we tend to be drawn toward black and white. We want to know what is true. We want to know exactly how to interpret a passage of Scripture. We want to know precisely what God is like and specifically what God's will is for our lives. We do not want to wonder or question. We do not want to trust or have faith. We simply want to know. We want certainty. The challenge for us as Christians is that faith does not involve certainty. Certainty is knowing beyond a shadow of a doubt. Faith is trusting despite uncertainty.

When I preach on a controversial issue, I try to lay out the views of Christians on both sides of the issue. Then I humbly offer my own thoughts on the issue, letting my listeners know that they do not have to agree with me. Inevitably people come up to me after the sermon and say, "Tell us how we are supposed to believe." I prefer to encourage others to think for themselves—to study the Scriptures, listen for the voice of the Spirit, find out what the church has to say, and use their own minds to bring all of this together in terms of understanding. The reality is that although some things in life are black and white with absolute certainty, many other things are gray. People see them differently. Encouraging people to look for the gray areas, think through issues, be open to new understandings, and accept those who think differently fosters faith and spiritual maturity. When we refuse to be open and to trust, division soon results.

70

Divisions That Separate Us

1. The Division of Denominationalism

When we insist on certainty, we often begin to think that we are right and those who disagree with us are wrong—and perhaps even evil. In the church, what tends to happen is that we become undone about small matters of doctrine and then divide over them. Wanting certainty when certainty cannot be found often causes us to over-simplify issues and polarize. This is why there is a long history among Christians of dividing and separating from one another. Today there are more than 3,000 different Christian denominations in America, and there are tens of thousands of non-denominational churches. Division results when we insist on seeing everything in black and white.

In the body of Christ, there are three major divisions: Roman Catholic, Orthodox, and Protestant. Of the two billion Christians in the world, one billion identify themselves as Roman Catholic, three hundred million identify themselves as Orthodox, and seven hundred million identify themselves as one of the many different Protestant denominations or non-denominational churches. Within these three major divisions, we have an interesting way of looking at one another. A couple of years ago the Vatican issued a statement clarifying how Catholics view non-Catholics. The statement was intended for Catholic theologians, not Protestants. Nevertheless, the clarifying words were that Protestants are wounded Christians who are defective in their faith, and that Protestant churches technically should not be called churches because they do not accept apostolic succession, the authority of the Pope, or a certain way of understanding the Eucharist. I must admit that after reading that statement, I felt slightly wounded by those remarks. Yet we all are guilty of wounding one another in the body of Christ.

A couple of years ago I interviewed an Orthodox priest for a sermon series I was preaching. I said, "I'm so glad to have a chance to meet with you. You belong to a part of the family of Christ that I'm not as familiar with, so please tell me about your part of the family."

He replied, "Well, for one thing, we are not in the same family."

I said, "Ah, so you mean we are not both Christians."

He responded, "Well, I don't know about you. But I'm not certain, that you all—actually, I'm certain that you are not a part of our family."

I said, "So let me get this straight. There are 300 million Orthodox Christians around the world, and there are 1.7 billion other Christians. And none of the rest of us are a part of Christ's family. So tell me, what's going to happen to the rest of us on the day of judgment?"

He said, "I don't know," which, I suppose, is better than saying, "You're all going to hell" but hardly comforting!

It is not only Orthodox and Catholics who wound their brothers and sisters in Christ. There are fundamentalist Christians who would say that anyone who worships in a Methodist or Lutheran or Episcopal church is not an authentic Christian. Likewise, there are moderate Christians who have said to me, "Pastor, please pray for my family. They are Catholics, and I really want them to become Christians." My first thought is, "Well, what are they now?" Is it not enough that Catholics call upon the name of Jesus, receive the sacraments, and profess faith in the same Apostle's Creed? Is it not enough that they call Jesus Lord and Savior, invite the Holy Spirit to work in their lives, seek to live a life of love, and read the Scriptures? Is there something else they need to do in order to be considered followers of Christ? Catholics may talk about their faith differently than Protestants, and some Catholics may be nominally religious—just as some Methodists and Baptists and Presbyterians are nominally religious. But I have met a tremendous number of Catholics who are deeply committed Christians. So, you see, all of us who call ourselves Christian have a way of wounding one other.

In John's Gospel we read that on the night before he was crucified, Jesus prayed, *"I ask not only on behalf of [my disciples], but also on behalf of those who will believe in me through their word. . . . that they may be one, as we are one"* (John 17:20, 22). Why did Jesus need to offer this prayer? Because he knew that differences would threaten to divide his followers.

When I think about the divisions within Christianity, I am reminded of the Pharisees. There must be times when God looks at us within the church and thinks, *When did you become Pharisees?* Jesus said, *"Woe to you, scribes and Pharisees, hypocrites! For you tithe mint, dill, and cummin, and have neglected the weightier matters of the law: justice and mercy and faith. It is these you ought to have practiced without neglecting the others. You blind guides! You strain out a gnat but swallow a camel!"* (Matthew 23:23-24).

Indeed, that is how we are. We tend to nitpick, straining out points of doctrine and dividing from one another. In the process, we miss the kind of life Christ actually called us to live. No longer do we pursue the things that are truly important. John Wesley, the founder of Methodism, said, "Would to God that all the party names, and unscriptural phrases and forms which have divided the Christian world, were forgot; and that we might all agree to sit down together, as humble, loving disciples, at the feet of our common Master, to hear his word, to imbibe his Spirit, and to transcribe his life into our own!"[1] Wesley's words describe beautifully what I mean by seeing gray. It is the capacity to look at people who are at different places theologically and spiritually than yourself and say, "You are still my brother or sister in Christ, and I have something to learn from you."

In my book *Christianity's Family Tree* (Abingdon, 2007), I take a look at eight different Christian denominations, pointing out what we can learn from each. There are things we can learn from the Pentecostal church about the Holy Spirit, for example, and things we can learn from the Catholic church about the importance of ritual, the role of reverence, and the power of the Eucharist. Rather than focus on our differences, we should be grateful for our Christian brothers and sisters and learn from them, just as we do in our biological families.

I have two daughters, Danielle and Rebecca, and they are as different as night and day. They think differently, they like different kinds of music and clothing styles, they have different tastes in boys, and they relate to me in very different ways. When they were little, they used to say to each other, "Daddy loves me more than you." Of course, that was not true. I love them the same. Even so, I treasure the fact that they are different and am grateful for their differences.

Seeing gray is the capacity to look at other people who disagree with us and say, "I might disagree with you, but I still love you. Instead of being undone by our differences, I'm going to listen and hear what you have to say; and maybe my own faith will be enriched and strengthened as a result." The ability to listen and learn from one another requires humility. When we humble ourselves, we are willing not only to listen and learn but also to serve others in humility—just as Jesus taught us to do.

The disciples often thought about which one of them would be the greatest in the Kingdom. They wanted to know which one of them Jesus loved more than the rest. James and John even sent their mom to go to bat for them. She asked Jesus to put one of them on his right and one of them on his left when he came into his kingdom. At the Last Supper, the disciples were once again arguing about who was the greatest, and Jesus demonstrated what it means to be great by getting down on his knees and washing their feet. In so many words he said, "The one who serves the most is the one who is greatest."

Serving others in humility demonstrates spiritual maturity. If you are not washing someone else's feet, figuratively speaking, do not bother thinking about how great you are in God's eyes or how spiritual you are.

One day the disciples came to Jesus and bluntly asked him who was the greatest in the kingdom of heaven. He answered them by calling a child to them and saying, *"Truly I tell you, unless you change and become like children, you will never enter the kingdom of heaven. Whoever becomes humble like this child is the greatest in the kingdom of heaven. Whoever welcomes one such child in my name welcomes me"* (Matthew 18:3-5).

The child did not understand the various theories of atonement and choose the right one. The child did not understand the various ways of interpreting the Scriptures and had not read them backward and forward many times. The child did not have a certain way of receiving the Eucharist or of understanding apostolic succession or icons or anything else. The child was humble and trusting. Whenever Jesus praised people and pointed them out as an example, they always were humble and trusting. He never praised anyone for Bible knowledge or good theology. He praised them for demonstrating the humility and faith of a child.

If we want to overcome denominational divisions, we must humble ourselves, listen, and learn from one another, and serve one another. As we do, we will grow in spiritual maturity.

2. The Division of Liberals vs. Conservatives

A second major division within Christianity is the split between liberals and conservatives. Actually, in some ways this division is more pronounced in the church than the division of denominations. Conservative United Methodists and conservative Catholics, for example, probably share more in common with one another than conservative and liberal United Methodists or conservative and liberal Catholics. Actually, this division has existed since the beginning of Christianity. In the early days of the church, conservatives and liberals were know as legalists and libertines. The first eight chapters of Romans, the third chapter of Philippians, the entire Epistle of Galatians, and most likely the Letter of James all were written to address the theological debate between the legalists and libertines.

The conservatives were called legalists because they were conserving the law. They held firmly to the Law of Moses, insisting that you had to obey all 613 laws, which included being circumcised if you were a man, in order to be a follower of Jesus Christ. Their reasoning was simply that following the law was the way they had always lived. The Scriptures said they had to obey the law, and that was it.

The liberals were called libertines because they said that Jesus set us free from the law. Because Jesus fulfilled the law, they argued that no longer was it necessary to follow the law. The old covenant had been marked "paid in full," and so they believed they were free to do whatever they wanted. If something felt right, it must be right. Thus, they acted upon their impulses. They did whatever felt good, thanking God for it and recognizing that they needed God's grace.

The apostles were neither legalists nor libertines. The apostle Paul taught that it was not necessary to be circumcised in order to be a follower of Jesus Christ. He explained that we are called to live a life that pleases God, and that the law is our guide that helps us to know the truth. Paul pointed out that Christ has indeed set us free from the law, just as the libertines said, but that we are not to use our freedom as an excuse for satisfying the lust of the flesh. Instead, we are to live a life worthy of the calling that we have received.

Paul stood right in the middle and tried to pull the two sides together. Basically, he said that both groups had some of the truth but not all of it. He taught that the truth is found in holding a careful balance between the two. Paul walked this balance between legalism and libertinism very carefully throughout all his epistles, calling for both faith and works.

At the beginning of the twentieth century, a great theological divide occurred along these same lines, creating the fundamentalists and the modernists, or liberals. This divide has shaped Christianity ever since, resulting in the culture wars we discussed in chapter 2. The debate between the two groups has largely been over their views of the Bible.

The modernists were led by a group of European seminary professors who had been influenced by the enlightenment. These professors began to ask questions of the Bible. They wanted to know if God actually instructed Moses to have the Levites slay 3,000 of their brothers and kinsmen and friends. *How does that fit in with the God of mercy we see in the New Testament?* they asked. They also wanted to know what to make of passages in the Bible where there seem to be discrepancies—contradictions with modern science or varying details in different accounts of the same story that cannot be reconciled.

The modernists concluded that the Bible is a library of writings penned by human beings over a period of 1,200 years, describing their reflections and thoughts and experiences of God; and as such, it carries a great deal of authority and weight for our lives. However, they saw the Bible as the words of human beings only. This was quite a liberating statement for them to make, because it allowed them to question and disagree with anything in the Bible. They could argue that a passage or a specific Scripture was written and intended for a particular time only—not for today. So, they began to question everything. The more radical among the modernists or liberals questioned every dogma and doctrine of the Christian faith, throwing out many of them.

This departure from traditional biblical scholarship created a strong reaction from Christians who were threatened by all the questions and uncertainty. As more and more modernists began to come to the seminaries here in American, there was a great stir in the mainline denominations—and ultimately in all of Christianity. Conservative Christians began to say, "Wait a minute. This is the Word of God, not the words of human beings." In keeping with Newton's third law of motion, which says that for every action there is an equal and opposite reaction, some conservatives reacted to the liberals' view of the Bible with an equally strong and opposite view. They said that every single word in the Bible was chosen by God and given to the prophets and apostles as if they were God's secretaries, writing down the things that God placed in their minds. They said that because every single word came from God, we cannot question any part of the Scriptures. If science disagrees with the Bible, then science is wrong. If we know that some dates in history do not align with the Bible, then the historians are wrong. Wherever we find discrepancies with science or other accounts, we must simply affirm that the Bible is perfect and right.

If, for example, the Bible says that the universe was created in seven days, then it was created in seven days. If it says that creation took place within the last 10,000 years, then it happened within the last 10,000 years. For these fundamentalists, there simply was no "wiggle room."

This rigidity of interpretation among conservatives began to move into other areas of church life. Some conservatives, for example, insisted that women are to keep silent in the church, just as the apostle Paul instructed. Of course, that instruction was written for a particular culture and time, and through the centuries we have come to a different understanding of the role of women. Today we recognize that women are co-creatures with men and, therefore, should have rights, such as being able to vote and to participate in leadership in the church. Extreme conservatives reacted to this liberal view, arguing that women should not even be allowed to be ushers because that would require them to talk in church. The most radical expressions of this interpretation gave women no rights whatsoever within the church.

Through the years, the debate between conservatives and liberals has gone back and forth in this manner. Conservatives say that because the Bible is God's revelation and the most important document for Christians, we should devote our time to studying the Bible, memorizing Scripture, and spending time in prayer. They say that the most important thing we can do is to win souls—to bring people to Jesus Christ. As a result, the focus in most conservative churches is leading people to a saving knowledge of Jesus Christ. For conservative Christians, Christianity is primarily about righteousness and holiness.

On the other side of the debate, liberals say that Christianity is more than saving souls; it is going out into the world to free people from oppression and bring about justice and righteousness. They contend that God wants us to be doers of the word, not just hearers, so they encourage us to focus on serving the poor and helping those who are needy. This, they argue, is what will help us to grow in our faith. For liberal Christians, Christianity is primarily about grace.

So, which group is right? That was the question I was wrestling with in 1987 when I was ordained as a pastor. I looked at the two groups and asked myself, "Are these my only choices—to be an extreme liberal or a radical fundamentalist? Or is there some middle ground?" For me and for millions of other Christians around the world, the truth is somewhere between the two extremes. We need holiness, but we also need grace. We need the social gospel, which calls us to address important issues in our world, but we lack the power to do anything of lasting value without the life-transforming message of personal salvation. The Bible was inspired by God, but it also was the work of human beings. This interplay between the divine and the human helps us to make sense of many challenging passages in the Bible. Rather than taking a black-and-white approach to Scripture, we need to allow a little bit of nuance in the middle.

I believe that if we only have the gospel represented by the conservatives, we have a faith that is imbalanced. Likewise, I believe that if we only have the gospel represented by the liberals, we have a faith that is imbalanced in the other direction. Ideally, if we can bring the two together, they will counter-balance each other, giving us a faith that captures the richness and fullness of who God is, what the Scriptures teach, and how Jesus Christ calls us to live. Seeking this place of balance is what I call seeing gray. It is a process that inevitably leads to spiritual maturity.

Fowler's Six Stages of Faith Development

Spiritual maturity—or faith development, as it sometimes is called—is, indeed, a process. In the classic, ground-breaking book *Stages of Faith* (Harper & Row, 1981), renowned psychologist and theologian James Fowler presented the idea of a developmental process in faith development. After conducting numerous in-depth interviews, Fowler determined that there is a correlation between an individual's psychological and spiritual development. He identified six stages of faith development that individuals may move through as they mature from infancy through adulthood. Briefly exploring these stages may help to deepen our understanding of spiritual maturity and its connection to our ability to see gray in a world of black and white.

Stages 1 & 2: Intuitive Projective Faith and Mythical Literal Faith

Let us consider stages and 1 and 2 simultaneously. Fowler said that these stages occur when we are first coming to faith as young children. When we are very young, we hear about God and even sense God, but we have a hard time differentiating between what is real and what is fantasy. We believe that God is a person we can see and touch, as is Santa Claus and the tooth fairy. Each is very real to us. Our beliefs are based on what we have been told by our parents or other adults. In these stages, faith is very literal.

Three or four times a year a little child will say to his or her parents as they approach me in our church, "There's God! There's God!" They say this because they see God as a person who wears a black robe and talks about spiritual things. On these occasions, I have the opportunity to clarify that view with them!

As we get a little older, we become capable of some differentiation, but our faith remains fairly literal throughout early childhood and the early elementary years. What we believe is largely based on what we have been told by our parents or Sunday school teachers.

Stage 3: Synthetic Conventional Faith

This stage may begin anywhere from the older elementary years to pre-teen or early teen years. In this stage, we begin to adopt the faith of our peers, who suddenly have become very important to us. As youth, we tend to adopt the views of the kids we hang around with, which is why our peer group is extremely important in the teen years. Adults other than Mom and Dad become very important as well. Spiritual teachers and mentors such as youth directors can have a significant influence. When we are teens, we will listen to a good youth director, for example, often embracing what we are taught without question. That happened for me.

When I was fourteen, I had a great youth director. Consequently, I began to read the Bible, to trust in Christ, and to follow him. As I listened to my youth director, what he taught became my faith. What my youth director said I should experience of the Holy Spirit was what I experienced of the Holy Spirit. How he interpreted the Bible was how I interpreted the Bible. How he dressed was how I tried to dress. I became a follower of my youth director, who was a follower of Jesus. That was my faith.

This kind of faith, however, is often unexamined. Generally we do not ask questions of it or dig deeper to see if it is true. It is not necessarily something we have owned. We have merely adopted it from someone else. Fowler says that some people never leave this stage of faith development.

Stage 4: Individuative Reflective Faith

This stage is a time of asking questions of our faith. Some of us never enter this stage; we have an unquestioning faith and never wrestle with our beliefs. We trust like a child, holding onto our faith all our lives. However, the majority of us begin to wrestle with our beliefs and wonder if they are true at some point in our lives. For those of us who mature early, this stage usually begins at age sixteen or seventeen, but typically it begins around eighteen when we are going away to college or leaving home. At this time in our lives, we are trying to differentiate ourselves from our parents, and often we reject much of what they taught us. Some of us give up our faith during this stage. We walk away from God. This is a normal part of faith development for some.

If this stage does not begin between the ages of eighteen and twenty-two, it often happens during a midlife crisis or a time of tragedy. Suddenly our unexamined faith no longer "fits" and we find ourselves saying, "Now where do I go?"

A mother whose three-year-old son was killed in a car accident wrote me this note about how that experience affected her faith:

I had had people tell me that it was my son's time. I was having a hard time believing in a God who would plan to take my child at age three. I learned that tragedies weren't necessarily a part of God's plan, but that God gave us free will and that sometimes bad things happen. Understanding this helped me to turn to God instead of away from him. Since my son's death, I believe that my faith has grown and continues to grow. His death changed the way I view God and my faith. I no longer have a naïve childlike faith where

God protects me from all harm and makes everything okay. It is a deep faith that has been tested through tragedy. I know that God doesn't promise me a pain-free life, but God does promise to always be there to love me, comfort me, and guide me. My faith gives me something that people without faith don't have—hope. Hope for the future. Hope in the knowledge that one day I will see my son again.

For me, the transition into this stage of faith development happened my first year of college when my youth director, who had led me to Christ, and his brother, who was my best friend, were both killed in a tragic accident. Suddenly I found myself questioning God. To that point in my life I had believed that if you loved Jesus and gave your heart to him, if you told other people about Jesus, if you tithed and went to church regularly, and if you read your Bible, then God would take care of you. But it didn't work out that way for the man who gave me that faith. So I began to think that maybe there is no God. Eventually I came to the point where I was able to see that God does not work in the simplistic way I had once thought. In the process of wrestling with my faith, my faith became stronger.

Stage 5: Conjunctive Faith

This stage is when we begin to be able to deal with paradox. Our faith becomes broader and wider than it has been before—it is no longer overly simplistic. At this stage we are able to deal with complexity and to hold things together that seem to be antithetical, recognizing that there is truth in more than one idea. We have the capacity to see the world with mystery and to realize that we will never understand everything there is to know about God—and this is okay. This recognition comes with a certain measure of humility and a great deal of grace.

I have heard people who have reached this stage say things such as, "The more I know, the more I realize I don't know" and "The longer I'm a Christian, the bigger God seems and the smaller my three pounds of gray matter seem." These individuals are better able to comprehend the mystery of God. They love and trust God and desire to know more about God and to follow God. They know they do not have it all figured out and never will.

One person who comes to my mind as a clear example of this stage of faith is Billy Graham. I have had the opportunity to visit briefly with Billy Graham on three different occasions. My strategy each time was to wait until everyone else in the group had left, and then I had a few minutes with him alone. What I observed in each of those three visits was his humility, grace, and willingness to see the world in broader terms than one might expect. My observation is affirmed by this remark made by Dr. Graham, which was quoted in an article that appeared in *Christian Century* several years ago:

I am now aware that the family of God contains people of various ethnological, cultural, class, and denominational differences. Within the true church there is a mysterious unity that overrides all divisive factors. In groups which in my ignorant piousness I formerly frowned upon, I have found men so dedicated to Christ and so in love with the truth that I have felt unworthy to be in their presence. I have learned that although Christians do not always agree, they can disagree agreeably. And that is what is most needed today. It is for us to show an unbelieving world that we love one another.

There was a time when Billy Graham invited Roman Catholics to be a part of the leadership team of his crusades. As a result, he lost a number of his followers. They refused to underwrite the campaigns, believing that he was compromising the gospel by allowing Catholics to be part of the crusades. Likewise, there was a time when he said he no longer would conduct crusades in the South unless blacks and whites could sit together in the same arena. If a city refused to agree to this request, then he refused hold a crusade there because he saw the world differently.

In 2006, Jon Meacham wrote a cover story on Billy Graham for *Newsweek* magazine. In the story Meacham noted the difference between Billy, who has softened over time, and his son Franklin, who tends to be a bit more conservative and fiery than his father. When asked about the difference between her father and brother, Ann Graham Lotz said, "When Daddy was my brother's age, he was saying some pretty strong things. But you have to remember that experience and the living of a life can soften your perspective." Experience softened him. It did not make him compromise; it caused him to see the world with broader eyes—to see the shades of gray—and to respond with grace and humility.

Reflecting on the man Billy Graham had become, Meacham wrote these words:

Billy Graham is an evangelist still unequivocally committed to the gospel, but he increasingly thinks God's ways and means are veiled from human eyes and wrapped in mystery. "There are many things I don't understand," he says. He does not believe that Christians need to take every verse of the Bible literally. "Sincere Christians," he says, "can disagree about the details of Scripture and theology." He says, "I'm not a literalist in the sense that every single jot and tittle is from the Lord. This is a little difference in my thinking through the years."

That is a monumental shift—to go from thinking that every jot and tittle in the Bible was placed there by God to allowing room for uncertainty. That is a picture of someone who has entered stage 5—who has the capacity to show humility and grace and to allow for mystery.

Fowler said that generally we do not reach this stage until we are forty years old, but I am finding that an increasing number of young people are reaching this stage. They do not want canned or pat answers to questions of faith. They are not interested in certainties. They do not believe it is an "either/or" kind of world but a world in which the truth is found somewhere between the two extremes. They are looking for an approach to the gospel that recognizes the gray areas.

Stage 6: Universalizing Faith

This stage involves emptying ourselves and focusing on God and other people. John Wesley described this process as sanctification. We seek to love God in every situation and to honor God above all else. No longer are we primarily concerned with ourselves and whether we are right and someone else is wrong. When we look at other people, our primary motivation is to express love to them. Although Fowler says that most of us will not reach this stage in this life, it is a stage we all should strive for.

In his first letter to the Corinthians, the apostle Paul was writing to a church that was divided. There were the charismatics who were speaking in tongues, and there were the social activists who were out caring for the poor. Both groups were looking down on each other, and the apostle Paul told them this was not how the gospel called them to live. The climax of his remarks comes in chapter 13. This part of the letter, known as the love chapter, was not written for weddings but for Christians who needed to know how to live. The chapter begins with familiar words:

> *If I speak in the tongues of mortals and of angels, but do not have love, I am a noisy gong or a clanging cymbal. And if I have prophetic powers, and understand all mysteries and all knowledge, and if I have all faith, so as to remove mountains, but do not have love, I am nothing. If I give away all my possessions, and if I hand over my body so that I may boast, but do not have love, I gain nothing. (vv. 1-3)*

Paul went on to describe what love looks like, because he wanted the Corinthians to know that love is a defining characteristic of a spiritually mature life. I invite you to read the following verses aloud, substituting your name every time you come to an underlined word. For example, "Adam is patient; Adam is kind. . . ." This is an excellent way to measure your spiritual maturity—how much you have conformed to what Christ longs you to be.

> *Love is patient; love is kind; love is not envious or boastful or arrogant or rude. It does not insist on its own way; it is not irritable or resentful; it does not rejoice in wrongdoing, but rejoices in the truth. It bears all things, believes all things, hopes all things, endures all things. (vv. 4-7)*

How did you do? What stage of faith development would you say that you are in currently? Regardless of your answers to these questions, remember that we all have room to grow and that faith development, or spiritual maturity, is an ongoing process.

A Final Challenge

The apostle Paul concluded 1 Corinthians 13 with words that are a fitting summary of spiritual maturity and an appropriate final challenge for each of us: *"And now faith, hope, and love abide, these three; and the greatest of these is love"* (v. 13). Spiritual maturity is trusting with childlike faith and loving God and others while never letting go of hope.

I challenge each of us to strive to grow in faith, hope, and love. May we place our trust in God and demonstrate our love for God and others, always holding firmly to the hope we have in Jesus Christ.

Notes

1. John Wesley, "Works Abridged From Various Authors by John Wesley," Vol. 14; pp. 237–238.

For Reflection and Response

1. Why do you think we tend to be uncomfortable with questions and uncertainty? Why does wanting certainty not always fit with faith?
2. What is the first major division that has separated Christians? What are its causes and its effects? Read John 17:11, 22-23. What was Jesus' prayer for us in these verses?

3. Read Matthew 23:23-24. How are we in the church often like the Pharisees as described in these verses? When have we strained out a gnat while swallowing a camel (focused on small matters while neglecting weightier issues)? Think of some specific examples.

4. How should we treat those who disagree with us? How can listening to what they have to say actually benefit us?

5. Read Matthew 18:1-5. What were the disciples concerned about? What did Jesus tell them? In what ways are we to be like children? What qualities or characteristics of children do we need in order to be spiritually mature?

6. What is a second major division within Christianity? How is this division evident within the church and the culture?

7. Many Christians believe that the truth lies somewhere between the right and the left, and that faith is imbalanced if it leans too far in either direction. Would you agree or disagree, and why? What does it mean to have a "balanced faith"?

8. What are Fowler's Six Stages of Faith Development? How would you describe the stage that most maturing Christians can hope to reach in this life? Do you know anyone who has reached stage 6?

9. Billy Graham has said that there is a mysterious unity within the true church that overrides all divisions. What does this mean? Do you agree that it is possible and necessary for Christians to "disagree agreeably"? Why or why not?

10. Read 1 Corinthians 13. According to these verses, what does love "look like"? How can these verses serve as a measuring stick for spiritual maturity?

5. What Would Jesus Say to America?

5. What Would Jesus Say to America?

I act with steadfast love, justice, and righteousness in the earth, for in these things I delight, says the LORD. . . . Thus says the LORD: Act with justice and righteousness, and deliver from the hand of the oppressor anyone who has been robbed. And do no wrong or violence to the alien, the orphan, and the widow, or shed innocent blood in this place. For if you will indeed obey this word, then through the gates of this house shall enter kings who sit on the throne of David, riding in chariots and on horses, they, and their servants, and their people. But if you will not heed these words, I swear by myself, says the LORD, that this house shall become a desolation. —Jeremiah 9:24; 22:3-5*

We live in a world in which there is so much polarization, especially in the area of politics. Sometimes it is difficult to have civil conversations about politics with even our closest friends if we do not agree with them. The world tends to think and operate in terms of black and white, yet as we have considered, things are not always black and white. There are shades of gray. My purpose throughout this book has been to help us focus on listening to one another, identifying the things that we can agree upon, and finding ways we can work together. We have considered how our faith can and should lead us in the areas of politics and morality. In this chapter we narrow the focus a bit more to consider what God has to say specifically about faith and government.

Three Hebrew Words

To begin the discussion, I would like to introduce three Hebrew words that are prevalent in Old Testament discussions about

Israel's system of government. The words identify three things that God expected of Israel's kings and leaders, because these words characterize or define who God is in the Old Testament.

Mishpat – Justice

The first word is *mishpat*, which appears 421 times in the Hebrew Bible. Typically this word is translated as "justice," although its meaning is actually broader and deeper. *Mishpat* is making sure that everyone receives what is fair, right, and equitable. It is doing the right thing by all people.

When we see the word *mishpat* or *justice* in the Old Testament, the reference generally is not to the elders or leaders of Israel, because they were the business owners, land owners, and kings—those individuals who had power and wealth. Usually the word makes reference to the disenfranchised or powerless—the poor, workers, children, widows, orphans, and aliens or foreigners. Again and again, God told those in power that they were to pursue *mishpat* so that all the people shared equitably. We see this throughout the Old Testament, particularly in the Law and the Prophets. Whenever the leaders of Israel were not ensuring that there was justice for all people, God would raise up prophets to warn them, saying essentially, "If you do not pursue justice, I will. I will execute justice in the land. And in the process, if you refuse to do it, I will see that your own nation falls." These were harsh words of warning for those leaders who would not pursue *mishpat*.

We find one of many examples in Psalm 146. We read,

> [The LORD] *executes justice* [mishpat] *for the oppressed;*
> *. . . gives food to the hungry.*

> The LORD sets the prisoners free;
>> the LORD opens the eyes of the blind.
> The LORD lifts up those who are bowed down;
>> the LORD loves the righteous.
> The LORD watches over the strangers;
>> he upholds the orphan and the widow . . . (*vv. 7-9*)

In these verses it is clear that justice means equity and fairness for all the people, including those who are not in power.

Tzedakah – Righteousness

The second important Hebrew word is *tzedakah*, which usually is translated "righteousness." Righteousness is more than moral behavior, such as refraining from using foul language or drinking excessively—although certainly these things might have been included in the meaning of righteousness. Generally Old Testament references to righteousness refer to doing the right thing at the right time in the right place for the right reason. This involves looking to God, who is the standard by which we determine what is right. Seeking righteousness is asking ourselves in every situation, "What is the thing that would please God?"

God not only expected his people to ask themselves this question; God also expected the nation's leaders to ask themselves this question about their policies and their form of governing. If they did not pursue righteousness, God promised that judgment or justice would come. In this way, the concepts of justice and righteousness were yoked together. God was saying, in effect, that righteousness and justice go hand in hand. We see this linking of righteousness and justice in the greeting that the Queen of Sheba gave to King Solomon. She indicated the specific role given to the king by God when she said, *"[God] has made you king to execute justice and righteousness"* (1 Kings 10:9).

Another way of thinking about righteousness is that it is doing the good or right or caring thing even when the law does not obligate you to do so. When you are righteous, you do the right thing not because the law mandates it—for example, not because there is a police officer waiting to write you a ticket—but because God demands it. Typically, this understanding of righteousness relates specifically to relationships with other people.

Hesed – Steadfast Love, Kindness, or Mercy

The third Hebrew word is *hesed*, which is translated "steadfast love, kindness, or mercy." *Hesed* is not a feeling but an action. Whether or not you *feel* love for someone else, you choose to *do* love toward the person. You act with kindness, even when the other person does not deserve it. Sometimes *hesed* is translated as "mercy." It is doing the kind thing even though others may be unloving or uncaring. You choose to love them steadfastly despite the fact that they are unlovable and do not merit your kindness.

Mercy is a defining characteristic of God. God continually shows us mercy and loving kindness despite the fact that we do not deserve it. Despite the fact that we sin and fall away, God continues to show us steadfast love, kindness, and mercy.

In the Gospels of Matthew and Luke, we see that Jesus spoke about this kind of love when he told us to love our enemies. Although the New Testament was recorded in Greek rather than Hebrew, the idea that Jesus was describing was essentially *hesed*. We are to show kindness to those who are our enemies. They do not deserve it, but we show them mercy anyway.

We see *hesed* linked with *mishpat* or justice in Micah 6:8, in which God says, *"What does the* LORD *require of you / but to do justice [mishpat], and to love kindness [hesed], / and to walk humbly with your God?"*

Why These Three Words Are Important

All three Hebrew words come together in Jeremiah 9:24: *"I act with steadfast love [hesed], justice [mishpat], and righteousness [tzedakah] in the earth, for in these things I delight, says the* LORD.*"* These three words define God, and they define what God expects of us in our relationships with one another. *Mishpat*, *tzedakah*, and *hesed* are what God demands of God's people in the nations, and what God expects the nations' leaders to pursue. The prophets warned that a nation who does not pursue these things will not stand. Again and again in the Old Testament, God promises that if we do these things, we will be blessed, but if we do not do these things, we will not stand. We hear this word of warning in Jeremiah 22:3-5:

> *Thus says the* LORD: *Act with justice and righteousness, and deliver from the hand of the oppressor anyone who has been robbed. And do no wrong or violence to the alien, the orphan, and the widow, or shed innocent blood in this place. For if you will indeed obey this word, then through the gates of this house shall enter kings who sit on the throne of David, riding in chariots and on horses, they, and their servants, and their people. But if you will not heed these words, I swear by myself, says the* LORD, *that this house shall become a desolation.*

God has asked us to pursue *mishpat, tzedakah,* and *hesed* as a nation. This is not a political party's issue; it is a national issue. These three words are a place where supporters of every political party can agree and come together. I cannot imagine anyone saying, "No, we do not want to pursue justice. We do not want to pursue what is right. We are not interested in kindness or mercy." We all agree on these things, regardless of our political party. Where we disagree is how we will administer them—what they will look like in particular situations.

For example, we all can agree that no child in America should go to bed sick because his or her family cannot pay for a doctor. Sick children need to be able to see a doctor, and we need to determine how to make sure that happens. We might disagree about how to make that happen, but we all can agree that it should happen because it represents *mishpat* and *tzedakah* and *hesed*. Likewise, we all can agree that employers should not abuse or oppress their workers. The question, of course, is how that should be addressed. Yet regardless of the how, we all can agree on fair treatment of employees because it represents *mishpat* and *tzedakah* and *hesed*. Certainly we all can agree that no one in America should starve to death. We may disagree about the root causes of the problem and the remedies, but we can agree about the need to do something to help those who are poor and hungry.

Imagine what could happen if we began to lock hands in our nation and say, "Let's pursue the things that represent *mishpat, tzedakah,* and *hesed*." Surely we would have different ideas and opinions, but we all could agree that these things are absolutely essential. In fact, they are part of our vision as a country.

The American Dream—Then and Now

Think for a moment about the vision of America—the American dream. How would you define it?

Today the American dream is popularly defined as being successful. For many, this means having a six-figure income, a 3,000 or greater square-foot house, and multiple cars. This was not the dream of the patriots who were willing to risk their lives for our country. For them, the American dream was much more noble. It included life and liberty and the pursuit of happiness, as well as other noble ideals.

The seal of the United States of America, found on the back of the one-dollar bill, represents the ideals of the original American dream. This two-sided seal was designed by Charles Thompson and approved by Congress in 1782. Let us take a look at both sides of the seal and consider the symbolism pertaining to the vision of our nation.

The Seal of the United States of America
1. The Great Pyramid

Source: Wikimedia Commons   Author: Ipankonin

First, there is the great pyramid. The pyramid represents strength and endurance. Just as the great pyramids have endured for thousands of years, so also America is a nation that endures. The pyramid is "undone" at the top to represent the fact that America's vision will never be completed. Every new generation is to work toward fulfilling that vision.

At the bottom of the pyramid is a scroll with the inscription *Novus ordo seclorum*, which means "the new order of the ages." The patriots believed that America represented something so new and profound and just and right that it would fundamentally change how nations and governments order themselves. This idea was expressed in many ways by the founding fathers, one of whom was Thomas Paine. In 1776, Paine wrote, "The cause of America is in great measure the cause of all mankind."

Above the pyramid are the words *annuit cœptis*, which is a Latin phrase meaning "favors our undertaking" or "looks with favor on our undertaking." This phrase both acknowledges the fact that someone looked with favor on the undertaking of America—on this new order of the ages—and expresses the hope that this someone will continue to look on America with favor. This someone is represented by the eye inside the triangle—the divine eye of providence or the all-seeing God. All of the founding fathers, including those who were not particularly religious, talked about God's providence and God's care in raising up this country and blessing the undertaking. Why? Because America stood for something that was important to God: justice, righteousness, and mercy or loving kindness. To the degree that we continue to walk along the path of these ideals, we continue to receive God's blessings and grace. But when we forget these things, we no longer receive God's favor.

2. The Eagle

The other side of the seal is an American bald eagle holding in its mouth a scroll that says *e pluribus unum*—"out of many one." This phrase refers to the fact that we are a nation of immigrants. Originally this part of the seal also had six

Source: Wikimedia Commons   Author: Ipankonin

small symbols representing the six nations from which most of the colonists had come. These small symbols served as a reminder that America was something unusual and different. America brought together people from other parts of the world who spoke different languages and had different faiths, yet out of many they became one.

Before we move on to other aspects of the seal, let us pause to reflect on the idea of many becoming one. One of America's greatest strengths has always been that we are a nation of people who see things differently—who come from different backgrounds bringing different heritages. This idea is captured in another great symbol of our nation, the Statue of Liberty. Lady Liberty stands in the harbor of New York, facing the nations of the world and welcoming people to America. She holds in her hand a torch of light as a reminder that America is a beacon of light to the nations, and as a message of welcome to those who come here from other lands. There is a poem called "The New Colossus," written by Emma Lazarus, inscribed on a bronze plaque inside the Statue of Liberty. As she stands at the harbor, Lady Liberty proclaims,

> Give me your tired, your poor
> Your huddled masses yearning to breathe free,
> The wretched refuse of your teeming shore.
> Send these, the homeless, tempest-tost to me,
> I lift my lamp beside the golden door!

All Americans, with the exception of the Native Americans, come from immigrant families. Even the Native Americans crossed a bridge during the Ice Age to become residents of this land. Each of us is here by the grace of God—and by the fact that someone welcomed us here.

This brings to mind the fact that that there are millions of other people wanting to come into our country today. How are we to handle this issue? I'm not certain of the answer, but I am certain of one thing: Whatever policies we come up with, they must treat aliens with *mishpat*, *tzedakah*, and *hesed*, because this is what God demands.

In the Book of Leviticus, God speaks this message again and again: "You, Israel, are to treat the foreigners in your midst in this way because you yourselves were foreigners and you were oppressed by the Egyptians. Therefore, don't do to them what was done to you. You are to treat them with justice and righteousness and *hesed*—loving kindness or mercy." This was not a political policy; it simply was the way that God wanted the people to address the issue. The same is true for us today. Our policies regarding immigration must incorporate the fundamental ideas of *mishpat*, *tzedakah*, and *hesed*.

Turning our attention back to the eagle, we come to the talons. One talon holds thirteen arrows, representing the militias of the thirteen colonies. In the other talon is an olive branch representing peace. On one hand, this symbolizes military strength, which is important for pursuing and maintaining peace. On the other hand, it serves as a reminder that peace is to be pursued. In fact, Charles Thompson talked about the arrows as symbols of the power of peace. He intentionally pointed the face of the eagle toward the olive branch to say that pursuing peace is to be our focus. Of course, it must be a just peace, and there are times that this requires military strength.

When we reflect on this part of the seal representing America's ideals, the challenge we face is how to balance military strength and the pursuit of peace. Military strength is important. Our soldiers try to administer justice and righteousness and mercy as best they can, and sometimes war becomes a necessary evil. We must be very careful, however, to ensure that war is always the last resort. After fighting the Revolutionary War, Benjamin Franklin said that he could not imagine any good war. His opinion was that war was to be avoided at all costs if possible. So, we must recognize that military strength and the pursuit of peace are both important, and we must continue striving to find the right balance between the two.

Our nation spends a significant amount of money on armaments and the military, some of which is necessary; but we spend a very small amount of money and time on diplomacy and humanitarian aid to those in other countries who need our help. In 2007, our military budget was six hundred billion dollars. That is more than all the other nations of the world combined spent on military expenses. China is second on the list for military spending, devoting 60 billion to the military in 2007.

To put it on a more personal level, 41 cents of every federal income tax dollar you send to the federal government goes to military expenditures. Only one penny goes to peace efforts—to diplomatic corps and humanitarian assistance for other nations. Again, military spending is absolutely necessary. The question I would like to raise is this: If we spent more money helping people through humanitarian aid in Third World countries, would we be able to decrease our military spending just a little because our own security might not be as threatened?

The BBC World Service Poll surveys tens of thousands of people around the world in forty-seven different countries to determine popular opinion regarding different nations and policies. In 1999, approximately 40,000 people in 27 countries were surveyed. The results indicated that a majority of people in most countries of the world perceived America as a positive force for good. Even among our enemies, the average person saw America as a positive force for good. Eight years later, in March 2007, 96,000 people in 47 countries were surveyed. Only 29 percent of people in those countries saw America as a force for good.

We long to be a force for good. That is, after all, how most of us picture our nation. Yet there is a difference between what we long to be and the way other countries perceive us. We should want other nations to admire America so much that they want to be like us, not only materialistically but also governmentally—in how they administer *mishpat, tzedakah,* and *hesed.* These three Hebrew words express God's vision for our nation. The question we must ask ourselves is this: How far have we strayed from these ideals in the operation and policies of our nation?

If Jesus Were to Address Our Nation

What would Jesus say if he actually came to America today in the flesh? If he walked among us, what would he say to us? As I reflected on these questions, I pictured in my mind Jesus standing on the steps of the Lincoln Memorial, addressing our nation. Before him was a multitude who had come to listen. They were hanging on every word, with microphones and television cameras capturing everything for posterity. I asked myself, *What would Jesus say to us? What questions would he raise?*

Some say that if Jesus were to come to America today, he would not talk about political issues at all. They suggest he would talk about how much he loves us, how much God loves us, and why he gave his life for us. I think he would indeed talk about those things. But is that all he would talk about? Would he say anything about the issues facing our nation? Would he say anything about immigration or abortion or homosexuality or health care or poverty or the environment or war? If so, what would he say? What things would he commend us for, and what things would he chastise us for?

I pondered these questions as I reflected on the Gospels of Matthew and Luke. I wondered whether Jesus would address the problems facing or nation or talk only about "spiritual things." After much reflection, I came to this conclusion: To God, everything is spiritual. Everything is in God's realm—how we make decisions, how we conduct business, how we relate to family and friends and coworkers, and how we govern our nation. All of these things have to do with our faith and the spiritual life.

When we read Jesus' words in the Gospels, we read statements such as, *"Blessed are those who hunger and thirst for righteousness [tzedakah], for they will be filled"* (Matthew 5:6). In other words, blessed are those who do the right thing in the right place at the right time for the right reason. They will be content. Likewise, Jesus said, *"Blessed are the merciful [hesed], for they will be shown mercy"* (Matthew 5:7). That is, those who show kindness, even when someone else does not deserve it, will be shown kindness and mercy.

Jesus also told parables, such as the parable of the rich man and the beggar, Lazarus, who died at his gates; the parable of the good Samaritan; and the parables of the sheep and the goats. When he was not preaching or teaching, Jesus spent much of his time healing the sick. He took time for those whom everyone else had turned away, making sure that they were cared for and made well.

Based on these observations of Jesus, I believe he would remind us that true greatness is not defined by our gross domestic product or our military might. I believe he would tell us that true greatness is seen in humility and servanthood and love. I think he would remind us of the things that children around the world pray about each night. Did you know that each night there are 30,000 children in the world who go to bed but do not wake up the next morning? Did you know that every thirty seconds a child in the Third World dies from malaria, which is a very curable disease in other parts of the world? Did you know that each night thousands of children in this country go to sleep in homeless shelters? Jesus sees and hears each of these children—as well as every adult who is hurting and in need. Knowing this makes me wonder what his heart must be for these people.

Some time ago, Richard Curtis, the head of Comic Relief, put together a moving video clip. He sent a cameraman to India with the instruction to video whatever he saw and bring back the images. The cameraman was setting up his camera when he saw a little girl in a yellow dress. Quickly he began to film her. In the video, the little girl, perhaps five years old, slowly and very carefully makes her bed on the sidewalk of a street of Calcutta, India, as pedestrians walk by. People walk right by the little girl and do not do anything. The end of the clip is the little girl going to sleep.

When I saw the video clip, it seized my heart. Jesus sees images like this all the time. The question for us is this: Would we walk by, or would we notice and stop to help? In Matthew 25, Jesus says in so many words, "*I was hungry. Some of you gave me something to eat, and some of you did not. I was thirsty. Some of you stopped to give me a drink while some of you walked right on by. I was naked and sick and in prison. Some of you helped, and some pretended not to see. Inasmuch as you pretended not to see, you will not be seen in the kingdom of heaven*" (Matthew 25:35-45, author's paraphrase).

A Challenge: Working Toward a Common Vision

We all see the world differently. As a result, there are many different ideas about the solutions to the problems in our nation and world. The starting point is to recognize the problems and to address them in light of the defining characteristics of our nation—those characteristics that are demanded by God and that make our nation great: *mishpat, tzedakah,* and *hesed.* The process is complicated, to be sure, and some conflict is unavoidable. But these three characteristics give us a firm foundation upon which to stand as we work together for a common vision.

One Friday night LaVon was out of town, and I asked three of my good friends to meet me at a local restaurant for dinner and a card game. Midway through the dinner I said, "Hey, let's talk about politics." As we talked about the issues, it was clear that we had very different opinions. We shared some things in common, but we all had different assessments of the problems and the solutions. At one point, the two who had the strongest opinions began to get louder, and you could feel the tension in the room. I began to wish I had not brought up the subject. Then I began to think about the fact that all four of us are really good friends who love each other and even attend the same church. We share in Bible study together and pray for one another. We all are followers of Jesus. Yet each of us holds very different views. Why? Because things are not always black and white. Some issues are complex and complicated. Even so, there are some things that all four of us can agree upon, and these include our desire to pursue justice and righteousness and mercy and loving kindness.

As we in our nation pursue this common vision of justice, righteousness, mercy, and loving kindness, we will have different ideas and strategies. The key to being able to work through these differences is to be able to look at one another and say, "We may disagree, but I still want to listen to you because you're my brother or sister."

My challenge to us as individuals and as a nation is to be people who offer our opinions with humility, recognizing that we might be wrong on some points; people who listen to one another; and people who try to work together toward common goals. My hope and prayer is that we will be people who can stand in the middle as a bridge, proclaiming that what is most important is that we pursue justice and righteousness and mercy and loving kindness.

As we begin to do these things, we will be taking steps toward becoming the kind of country that inspires other nations—not by our military might, but by our compassion and generosity and sense of justice for all. In the process, we will come to recognize that sometimes the truth is found on more than one side of an issue—sometimes there are shades of gray in a world of black and white.

For Reflection and Response

1. What is the meaning of *mishpat, tzedakah,* and *hesed*? What do these three Hebrew words tell us about God and what God expects of us?
2. Read Jeremiah 22:3-5. What did God ask of the people? What did God say would happen if they obeyed and if they did not?
3. Why do you think God calls leaders and those in power to ensure that everyone gets what is fair and equitable?
4. If righteousness is doing the right thing at the right time in the right place for the right reasons, how would you rate our nation

in the area of righteousness, and why? How would you rate yourself?

5. What is challenging or difficult about showing *hesed*—mercy or loving kindness?

6. Read Micah 6:8. If we were truly to live according to this verse, what kind of changes would take place in our families, schools, workplaces, churches, and government?

7. How does the American dream as popularly understood today differ from the original American dream of our nation's founders? What new insights regarding the ideals of our nation do you have after learning about the symbolism of the seal of the United States?

8. What are some of the challenges we face as a nation in balancing military strength with the pursuit of peace? How successful do you think we have been in this effort, and why?

9. If Jesus were to address America today, what do you think he would say? What would he commend us for? What would he chastise us for?

10. Read Matthew 25:31-46. According to these verses, what does Jesus want us to be focused on as individuals, communities, and a nation? How are you involved in meeting the needs of others in your own community and beyond? What needs has God placed most heavily on your heart?

11. What can we do to pursue a common, unified vision as a nation despite our disagreements?

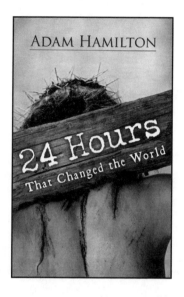